H
Chef Val

Personal Chef
Secrets

Personal Chef Val Greenlaw

Copyright © 2004 by Home Chef

Published by Home Chef
4500 W. Hinsdale Avenue
Littleton, CO 80128
(303) 972-4986
www.homechef.net
Email: personalchefsecrets@yahoo.com

Library of Congress Control Number: 2004104594
ISBN: 0-9752949-0-3
First Edition

Printed in the USA by: Bang Printing
3323 Oak Street, Brainerd, MN 56401
www.bangprinting.com

Book Design, Cover Design, and Layout:
Dale Stebbins of Stebbins Advertising & Design, Inc.
www.stebbinsadvertising.com

Photography: Andy Ledbetter

Editor: Val Greenlaw

Dedication

••

To my Family and Friends that have endured years of tasting my many recipes goes a special thank you.

To Mom and Dad there are not enough words to express the love and gratitude I feel for you. Thank you for always encouraging me to be the best and to never give up.

To my clients, thank you for your patience and honest comments, without you this cookbook would not have been possible.

To Jolaine Harbour, my ja ja Sister, thank you for encouraging me to dream and have the courage to follow my dreams.

And finally to the man who is the beneficiary of many of my culinary creations and is always honest, thank you John for your unending support. I love you!

Thank you God for the talent you have blessed me with!

Chef Val

Contents

Introduction

O ver the years of collecting and developing recipes, I realized there are some very important processes, tips, and thoughts that I have incorporated into my cooking techniques. These techniques are important to the success of any cook, yet they haven't found a spot in the actual recipes contained in this cookbook. So I thought I would take a few minutes to review with you what I think are important tips that will help you be a better cook.

Usually, I spend one day a week researching and planning menus for the next week. Now you think you don't have the time, but if you spend an hour thinking about next week's meals you'll find you're less stressed throughout the week and have more time. During this planning time I make a list of all the ingredients I need for each recipe. Then I go into my pantry, freezer, and refrigerator and determine what I have on hand, checking off each ingredient from my master list. Now I have a grocery list and proceed to purchase what I need all at once. Upon arriving home I follow Rachael Ray's philosophy. I clean everything before placing it in the refrigerator. Boy does this save time!

In preparing for a recipe or menu for my clients or family, I make sure to
• read through the entire recipe before beginning,
• gather all the ingredients,
• do all the chopping and measuring prior to beginning the cooking process.

Additionally, I try to make all my own seasoning blends. This allows me to control the various ingredients, but more importantly; the freshness. In fact I buy most of my spices in bulk, filling smaller spice bottles as needed and then using the smaller spice bottles on a day to day basis. The bigger spice bottles are stored on my freezer door. This keeps them fresh. If you don't know where to look for recipes for these blends, check out www.google.com and I'm sure you'll find what you are looking for.

I also discovered that brining chicken, turkey, and pork really does improve the flavor and helps maintain tenderness. Brining is soaking the poultry or pork in a salt solution for a specific period of time. You might want to review the Brining recipe in this cookbook for specific details. Because of this I am forced to plan these types of meals ahead of time, allowing for adequate brining.

When reading the recipes in this book, you might notice "(see recipe)" in the ingredients list. This indicates that the recipe for this item can be found in this cookbook. Check out the index and locate the recipe for the item.

There are several cookbooks and magazines that I can't live without and I thought I would share them with you and hope that they too will contribute to your success in the kitchen:

Food Lover's Companion – This is full of culinary definitions and items you aren't sure of.

Culinary Artistry – This helps pair various types of foods with other ingredients or food items.

Martha Stewart's Hors D'oeuvres Handbook – This book is great when trying to decide upon appetizers.

Sauces by James Peterson – Every type of sauce you can image are detailed in this book.

Rachael Ray's 30 Minute Meals 2 – Great collection of tasty yet fast meals.

The Complete Meat Cookbook – Wonderful descriptions on the various cuts of meat and how to cook them.

Magazines – Cooking Light, Gourmet, Bon Appetite, Fine Cooking

I hope that you find the recipes in this book delicious and that you'll find this collection one you'll use <u>again and again.</u> Most importantly it will make <u>you look like a pro</u> to your families and friends as a result of cooking the many recipes in this book.

Happy Cooking and God Bless,

Chef Val

Chocolate
Cheesecake
with Hot
Fudge Sauce

About the
Author

C hef Val Greenlaw grew up as a military daughter, traveling around the world and experiencing many types and styles of food. After her father completed a 3 year tour of duty in Germany, the family was transferred to the Washington D.C. area. This is where she began her true passion for cooking. It started first with simple recipes and modifications of ready packed foods. To this day her Mother can not eat Macaroni and Cheese from the box.

Also during this time Chef Val became extremely interested in the computer industry, taking 4 hours of computer science classes in high school. After graduating she went on to Virginia Tech and completed her BS in Computer Science. It was here that she met her roommate, Anne Prince. Anne grew up in southern Virginia and brought new culinary experiences that encouraged Chef Val to be more experimental in the kitchen. You'll find several simple recipes Anne shared with Chef Val included in this cookbook.

Chef Val left Virginia for Colorado and began a career selling Hewlett-Packard Technical Computers. It is here that she married and began her own household. Then after 5 years she and her husband and two dogs moved to California. California offered so many options in pleasing the palette and also offered affordable cooking classes specializing in different styles of foods.

Once in California, Chef Val left Hewlett-Packard and went to Silicon Graphics. Here she ran many different marketing departments and began to experiment with baking in a much bigger way. She always baked for her employee's birthdays, hosted department dinners, or arranged unique department cooking classes to bring her staff together as a team in a new and unique way.

Then came the 90's, hard times for computer companies with multiple companies laying people off. Chef Val left Silicon Graphics to take on several consulting jobs before landing at Apple Computer, working directly for Steve Jobs as the Director of Higher Education.

This was a very challenging job and gave her a new appreciation for brand awareness and brand protection. After 16 months on the job another layoff forced her to find another opportunity. She took a job as Senior Director of Higher Education at edu.com, a new dot-com company based out of Boston.

After edu.com blew through several millions of dollars of IPO money, they closed up shop like many of the dot-coms. It was at this time that Chef Val realized she wasn't as happy as she thought she was and started investigating other career options. It was after this soul searching that she decided to follow her passion for cooking.

Chef Val decided to join the American Personal Chef Association (APCA) and began to pull together her very own Personal Chef business. She named her business the Home Chef and took as many cooking classes as possible at Cook Street School of Fine Cooking in Denver, Colorado. It was here that she fine tuned her skills and became extremely food oriented. She went to the seminars and classes offered through the APCA.

Her personal chef clients and many dinner party clients helped Chef Val to develop a repertoire of great meals that have to be prepared easily since she cooks all 20 meals in clients' homes in less than 4 hours.

It was at her friends and clients prodding that Chef Val decided to gather her collection of recipes and publish a cookbook for the everyday home cook. These recipes have been tested and used over the past 22 years.

Chef Val hopes that you enjoy these recipes, tips, and secrets and will find this cookbook a valuable part of your cookbook collection.

Bon Appétit,

Chef Val

Appetizers & Light Meals

Asparagus Straws

∙∙∙

Asparagus Straws

1 bunch asparagus spears – trimmed
1 box phyllo dough – thawed
1 stick butter – melted
½ cup parmesan cheese

Steam asparagus until just al dente and bright green. Transfer to a cookie sheet to cool.

Preheat oven to 450°. Line baking sheets with silpat sheets.

Take 1 sheet of phyllo and place on a smooth surface. Brush phyllo with melted butter. With a pizza cutter, divide phyllo into 4 rectangles. Place asparagus spear at one end of the rectangle with tip exposed beyond phyllo edge. Then sprinkle with parmesan and roll up. Place finished straw on baking sheet. Continue process until all spears are completed.

Before baking brush straws with butter and then sprinkle with cheese. Cover the tips of the asparagus with foil to protect them from burning.

Bake until golden brown 8-10 minutes. Serve warm or at room temperature.

Asparagus & Ham Mini Quiches

1 bunch asparagus
½ cup milk
½ cup heavy cream
2 large eggs
1 large egg yolk
⅛ teaspoon freshly grated nutmeg
5 ounces gruyere cheese – finely shredded
5 ounces cooked ham – cut into ¼" squares
1 Pie Crust (see recipe)

Make the pie dough. Let rest in the refrigerator for 1 hour.

Bring a pot of water to a boil. Salt liberally, and then add the asparagus. Cook until just tender. Immerse in an ice bath, and then drain well. Cut into ¼" to ½" pieces.

Dice the ham and shred the cheese. Set aside. In a medium bowl, whisk together milk, heavy cream, eggs, yolk, and nutmeg. Season with salt and pepper. Strain through a sieve into a medium bowl. Pour this mixture into a pitcher or measuring cup with a spout. This will make it easier to pour into the mini-muffin cups.

On a slightly floured surface roll out the dough to slightly less than ⅛" thick. Using a 2¼" round cookie or biscuit cutter, cut out 48 rounds. You may need to cut the dough into smaller pieces to roll out on the size surface you have. The scrapes can be kneaded together and used once more.

Spray your mini-muffin pans with cooking spray, then center the dough round over the muffin cups, using a tart tamper or your fingers, gently push the dough into the muffin hole. Repeat this process until all the muffin cups are filled.

Place the dough filled muffin tins in the refrigerator to rest for 15 minutes.

Reserve ½ cup of the cheese and set aside.

Divide the cheese evenly between the lined muffin cups. Top with the chopped ham and asparagus. Then pour the egg-milk mixture evenly between the cups. Sprinkle with the remaining cheese.

Bake until puffed and golden brown, approximately 30 minutes. Remove from the oven and immediately remove quiches from the muffin tin and transfer to a wire rack.

Serve warm or at room temperature.

Artichoke & Cherry Tomato Tarts

1 large egg yolk – beaten
¼ cup sour cream
1 sheet frozen puff pastry – thawed,
   cut into 2" squares
1 cup quartered, marinated artichoke
   hearts – drained
10 vine-ripened cherry tomatoes – halved
1 teaspoon fresh thyme leaves (optional)

Preheat oven to 400°. Lightly flour a baking sheet.

In a bowl, whisk together yolk and sour cream, season with salt and pepper. Place pastry squares on baking sheet and spoon 1 teaspoon of the egg mixture onto center of each. Using the back of the spoon spread the mixture evenly. Divide the artichokes and tomatoes evenly between the puff pastry squares. Spoon remaining sour cream mixture, 1 to 2 teaspoons, over vegetables. Sprinkle with thyme.

Bake in oven until pastry is golden, about 12 minutes.

Best Margaritas

1¾ cups Cuervo Gold Tequila
¼ cup Grand Marnier
¼ cup Cointreau
5 tablespoons simple sugar syrup
1 cup fresh squeezed lime juice

Put all ingredients into a blender filled ¾ full of ice and blend.

Bourbon-Bacon Scallops

3 tablespoons green onions – minced
2 tablespoons bourbon
2 tablespoons maple sugar
1 tablespoon low-sodium soy sauce
1 tablespoon Dijon mustard
¼ teaspoon pepper
1½ pounds large sea scallops
6 slices low sodium bacon
cooking spray
toothpicks, soaked in water

Combine first 6 ingredients in a bowl; stir well. Add scallops, stirring gently to coat. Place in a Ziploc baggie and marinate in refrigerator overnight. Turning several times.

Remove scallops, reserving marinade. Cut each slice of bacon into 4 pieces (lengthwise, then in half). Wrap 1 bacon piece around each scallop. Use a toothpick to secure the bacon around the scallop.

Spray baking sheet with cooking spray. Place scallops on cookie sheet; broil 8 minutes or until the bacon is crisp and scallops are done. Baste occasionally with the reserved marinade.

Tips from Chef Val

Instead of crackers try Bagel Chips! Cut the bagels into thin slices, place on a baking sheet, bake at 350° for 5 minutes.

Cathy's Hot Artichoke Dip

2 14 ounce cans artichoke hearts – quartered
2 cups mayonnaise
2 cups parmesan cheese
1 cup plain yogurt
1 bunch green onions – chopped
Italian bread crumbs
salt and pepper

Heat oven to 350°.

Combine all ingredients except bread crumbs. Taste for seasoning and add salt and pepper according to taste. Pour into oven proof dish. Sprinkle top with bread crumbs and bake for 30 minutes or until golden brown.

Serve with crackers or chips.

Clam Dip

2 8 ounce packages cream cheese
½ cup mayonnaise
6 ounce jar chili sauce
2 6½ ounce cans clams – minced

Bring cream cheese to room temperature. Drain and wash clams.

Mix cream cheese, mayo, and chili sauce until well combined. Then add clams and mix to distribute.

Serve with tortilla chips.

MENU IDEAS

Hors D'oeuvre Party

Salmon Mousse
Bourbon-Bacon Scallops
Brie & Garlic Crostini
Tomato Pesto & Bagel Chips
Cranberry Biscuits with Ham
Eggplant Spread and Crackers
Clam Dip and Chips
Artichoke & Cherry Tomato Tarts

Appetizers & Light Meals

· ·

Chicken & Cheddar Empanaditas

1 cup Granny Smith apples – cored, peeled,
   and diced
2 tablespoons lemon juice
2 tablespoons butter
1 cup red onion – finely chopped
4 cloves garlic – minced
2 8 ounce chicken breasts – boned, skinless
1⅓ cups white cheddar cheese – grated
1½ tablespoons fresh rosemary –
   finely chopped
salt and pepper
1 large egg
1 tablespoon milk

Empanada Dough
3¾ cups flour
¾ teaspoon salt
6 tablespoons vegetable shortening
12 tablespoons butter
½ cup ice water
2 tablespoons ice water

Toss the diced apples with the lemon juice and set aside.

Cut chicken into thin strips. Set aside.

In a medium skillet over medium heat melt the butter. Then add the onions and garlic. Cook for about 8 minutes or until soft. Add the apple mixture and cook for about 5 minutes or until the apples are soft. Then add the chicken and turn up the heat to medium high. Cook until the chicken is cooked through, about 5 minutes. When chicken is done transfer mixture to a bowl and cool.

Shred the chicken into small pieces. Stir in the rosemary and cheddar cheese. Add the salt and pepper to taste.

Empanada Dough: In a food processor, combine the flour, salt, and sugar. Then add the vegetable shortening and butter.

Pulse until the mixture resembles coarse meal. With the machine running add the cold water through the feed tube and pulse until the dough forms a ball. Transfer the dough to a piece of plastic wrap. Wrap the dough and place in a Ziploc baggie. Refrigerate for 1 hour.

Preheat the oven to 375°.

Roll the dough out to a thickness of ⅛". Using a 3" biscuit or cookie cutter, cut out 50-60 circles. Place the rounds on a greased cookie sheet or one lined with parchment paper. Cover with plastic and refrigerate for 30 minutes. In a small bowl lightly beat the egg and milk together. Set aside.

Place a tablespoon or an amount of filling that allows for the dough to close over the filling. Place the filling a little off center, brush water around rim, then fold the circle in half, forming a half moon. Pinch the edges together with your fingers. Use a fork to seal the dough. Brush the tops with the egg wash and place on the cookie sheet. Continue until all the filling is used.

Bake until the dough is golden, 15 to 20 minutes. Serve warm.

If you don't need all of the empanaditas for your menu, you can freeze these individually on the cookie sheet, then transfer them to a Ziploc baggie and store in your freezer for up to 3 months. Then bake them frozen for 30 minutes.

NOTE: You can make this into empanadas by cutting the dough into 5" to 6" circles and using more filling per circle.

....

Brie & Garlic Crostini

1 baguette – sliced ½" thick
½ cup Roasted Garlic (see recipe)
1 wedge brie – sliced ¼" thick
½ cup olive oil

Set oven to broil. Cut baguette into ½" slices. Using a pastry brush, brush the olive oil on each piece, turn over and brush with remaining olive oil. Place slices on a cookie sheet and broil in oven for 4 minutes or until browned. Turn over and brown. Don't take your eyes off these as they can burn quickly depending on the temperature of your oven. Remove slices to a wire rack to cool.

Take Roasted Garlic and place into a food processor. Process until smooth and resembles a paste.

Spread 1½ teaspoon of garlic on each slice, top with a slice of brie. Place slices on cookie sheet and broil in oven until cheese just melts, about 4 minutes.

Serve immediately.

Egg Salad

8 Perfect Hard-Boiled Eggs (see recipe)
½ cup mayonnaise
¼ celery – finely chopped
2 teaspoons Dijon mustard
hot sauce
salt and pepper

In a medium bowl combine all ingredients. I use an egg slicer in both directions to finely chop the eggs. Salt and pepper to taste after all other ingredients are combined. Serve over salad or as a sandwich.

Eggplant Spread

1 large eggplant
¼ cup olive oil
1 medium green pepper – chopped
1 medium onion – chopped
1½ teaspoons garlic – minced
1 cup fresh mushrooms – chopped
1 6 ounce can tomato paste
½ cup water
2 tablespoons red wine vinegar
2 teaspoons sugar
½ teaspoon salt
½ teaspoon dried oregano
¼ teaspoon pepper

Peel eggplant, cut in half, then dice. Measure out 3 cups. Set aside.

Heat oil in skillet over medium heat; add 3 cups of eggplant, green pepper, onion, and garlic. Cover and cook, stirring occasionally for 15 minutes. Add mushrooms and next 7 ingredients; bring to a boil. Cover, reduce heat and simmer, stirring occasionally for 15 minutes or until eggplant is tender. Cool slightly, cover, and chill for at least 2 hours.

Serve with crackers.

Salmon Mousse

¾ pound salmon fillet
1 14½ ounce can vegetable broth
1 cup milk
1 slice onion
6 peppercorns
1 bay leaf
pinch mace
1 tablespoon butter
1 tablespoon flour
2 tablespoons butter
2 tablespoons cream
2 tablespoons dry sherry

Place the salmon in a skillet, then pour the vegetable broth over. Over medium to low heat poach the salmon. Allow to cool in the liquid, then remove any skin or bones.

Place the milk, onion, peppercorns, bay leaf, and mace in a saucepan. Cover and set on a low heat for 5-7 minutes. Do not boil. Strain the milk.

In a skillet combine the 1 tablespoon of butter and flour. Pour in ⅓ cup of the milk and mix until well combined. Add the remaining milk. Season with salt and pepper. Heat slowly and stirring continually until boiling. Boil for 2 minutes. Cool.

Cream 2 tablespoons butter until soft. Half whip the cream. Break the salmon into pieces and grind into small pieces with a fork. Place the salmon in a mixing bowl, slowly add the milk sauce. Fold in the butter, cream, and sherry. Do not overwork this mixture.

Pour into a decorative mold, smooth over the top, cover with plastic wrap, and place in the refrigerator until firm.

Remove from refrigerator, loosen mold. If it doesn't release, run a knife around the edge of the mold. Invert onto serving plate and serve with crackers.

Spinach Dip

8 ounce package cream cheese
3 ounces mayonnaise
1 teaspoon cornstarch
½ teaspoon Tabasco sauce
¼ teaspoon kosher salt
2 cups parmesan cheese
4 ounces fresh spinach – chopped
2 ounces sour cream
¼ cup yellow onion – julienned
½ teaspoon fresh garlic – minced
1 ounce roasted red pepper – julienned
4 ounces artichoke hearts – quartered

Mix ingredients together and bake at 450° for 10 minutes, or until golden brown.

NOTE: You can add bay shrimp or crab meat if desired.

Party Pumps

1 cup monterey jack cheese
1 cup cheddar cheese
½ cup chopped black olives
½ cup mayonnaise
dash curry
½ teaspoon garlic powder
1 loaf party pumpernickel

Mix first six ingredients. If too dry add more mayonnaise a little at a time.

Spread on bread. Bake for 10 minutes in a 350° oven.

Serve hot.

Hummus

4 cloves garlic
2 15 ounce cans garbanzo beans – drained
1½ teaspoons salt
⅓ cup tahini
6 tablespoons lemon juice – freshly squeezed
2 tablespoons water or liquid from the
   garbanzo beans
8 dashes hot sauce

In a food processor, process the garlic. Add the remaining ingredients until smooth. Taste for seasoning and serve chilled with pita bread.

Open Face Turkey Sandwich

4 slices country bread
4 teaspoons low-fat mayonnaise
4 teaspoons Dijon mustard
1 cup arugula – trimmed
4 slices red onion – ⅛" thick
12 ounces thinly sliced deli turkey
2 apples – cored and cut crosswise
   into ¼" slices
½ cup havarti cheese – grated
salt and pepper

Preheat broiler with oven rack in middle position.

Spread each bread slice with 1 teaspoon mayonnaise and 1 teaspoon mustard. Layer each slice with ¼ cup arugula, 1 onion slice, 3 ounces turkey, 4 apple slices, and 2 tablespoons cheese.

Place sandwiches on a baking sheet; broil 4 minutes or until cheese is bubbly. Remove from heat; sprinkle with salt and pepper.

Shrimp Egg Rolls

1 tablespoon canola oil
2 cups frozen cooked shrimp – thawed,
   finely chopped
⅓ cup green onions – sliced
½ cup canned bean sprouts – chopped,
   well drained
1 tablespoon minced water chestnuts
1 tablespoon soy sauce
1 teaspoon fresh ginger root – grated
¼ teaspoon salt
⅛ teaspoon white pepper
1 egg – slightly beaten
10 egg roll wrappers – 5 to 6 inch squares
canola oil – for deep frying
1 Sweet & Sour Sauce (see recipe)

In a large skillet heat the oil over medium heat. Stir fry the shrimp and green onion until golden, 2 to 3 minutes. Add bean sprouts, water chestnuts, soy sauce, ginger root, salt, and white pepper. Heat for 1 minute. Remove from heat. Set aside to cool. Stir beaten egg into shrimp mixture.

Spread 2 tablespoons filling along 1 side of each egg roll wrapper, leaving ½" uncovered on each end. Then fold sides in and begin to roll. Dip fingers into water and moisten the end of the egg roll, pressing to seal the edge.

Cover completed egg rolls with plastic wrap to prevent drying out. Heat deep-frying oil to 365°. Deep-fry the egg rolls in the hot oil until surface is crisp, bubbly, and golden, 3-4 minutes.

Serve with Sweet & Sour Sauce.

NOTE: You can freeze these uncooked in a Ziploc baggie for up to three months.

. . . .

Tomato Pesto

2 28 ounce cans diced tomatoes – drained
½ cup Roasted Garlic (see recipe)
½ cup shallots – finely chopped
⅛ cup white balsamic vinegar
¼ cup basil – finely chopped
¼ cup parsley – finely chopped
1 to 2 cups olive oil
salt and pepper – to taste

Place tomatoes and all but the olive oil in the food processor. Process until no tomato chunks remain. With processor on, slowly pour in ¼ cup of oil. Check taste and add up to 2 cups of oil, ¼ cup at a time. Make sure to season with salt and pepper.

Serve with sliced bread or bagel chips.

Soups, Salads, & Dressings

Arugula and Orange Salad with
Poppyseed Dressing

Soups, Salads, & Dressings

Anne's Cole Slaw Dressing

1 cup mayonnaise
½ cup sugar
¼ cup vinegar

Combine all ingredients with a whisk. Pour over shredded cabbage. Refrigerate. Mix before serving and serve with a slotted spoon.

Arugula & Orange Salad with Lemon Vinaigrette

4 cups arugula
1 11 ounce can mandarin oranges
1 red onion – shaved
juice of one lemon
1 tablespoon sugar
⅓ cup red wine vinegar
½ cup canola oil
½ cup olive oil
2 cloves garlic – minced or pressed
salt and pepper – to taste

Combine arugula, oranges, and red onion in salad bowl. In a Mason jar with a lid or blender, mix together lemon juice, sugar, vinegar, garlic, salt, and pepper. Shake or blend well. Add oils. If using blender add oils slowly. Toss salad with dressing and serve.

Blue Cheese Coleslaw

½ cup blue cheese – crumbled
½ cup buttermilk
3 tablespoons apple cider vinegar
2 tablespoons sugar
1 head green cabbage – shredded

Place cheese, milk, vinegar, and sugar in a food processor. Blend until smooth, about 1 minute.

Place shredded cabbage in a large bowl. Add the dressing. Toss and season with salt and pepper. Cover and chill at least 1 hour.

Balsamic-Port Dressing

½ cup Port wine
⅓ cup balsamic vinegar
1 tablespoon honey
1 tablespoon fresh thyme – finely chopped
¼ cup shallot – chopped
2 tablespoons Dijon mustard
2 tablespoons extra virgin olive oil
¼ teaspoon salt
freshly ground black pepper

Combine Port, vinegar, honey, thyme, and shallot in a small saucepan. Bring to a boil over medium-high heat. Reduce heat to low and simmer, uncovered for 5 minutes.

Remove from heat; strain through a fine mesh wire strainer. Whisk in mustard, oil, salt, and pepper.

Serve warm or at room temperature. If storing save in a Mason jar and shake well before serving.

Crab or Lobster Stew

2 tablespoons butter
6 small soda crackers
2 cups crabmeat or lobster meat
½ cup water
1 quart milk
salt and pepper
1 12 ounce can evaporated milk

Melt butter slowly in kettle in which you are to make the stew. In a blender, food processor, or food chopper place the crackers and grind until fine as a flour. Place cracker crumbs and crabmeat in the butter. Add water and let this bubble for 1 minute. Pour in fresh milk and stir constantly until small bubbles appear on the surface. Do not boil. Season to taste with salt and pepper. Then add the evaporated milk. Let this come to a simmer. Do not boil.

Serve immediately.

Soups, Salads, & Dressings

Black Bean & Corn Salad with Zesty Lime Vinaigrette

3 tablespoons freshly squeezed lime juice
1½ tablespoons extra virgin olive oil
hot sauce – to taste
¼ teaspoon garlic salt
1 15 ounce can black beans – rinsed
  and drained
1 cup frozen corn – thawed and drained
1 tomato or ½ cup canned diced tomatoes –
  seeded, drained, and chopped
¼ cup red onion – finely chopped
½ cup soy beans
2 tablespoons fresh cilantro – minced

In a bowl, whisk together first 4 ingredients.

In a medium bowl combine remaining ingredients. Pour vinaigrette over veggies and stir to combine. Cover and let stand for at least 20 minutes. Serve at room temperature.

Honey French Dressing

¼ cup red wine vinegar
2 tablespoons ketchup
¼ cup honey
¼ cup sugar
¼ teaspoon sea salt
1 teaspoon freshly ground pepper
½ teaspoon celery seed
1 teaspoon paprika
1 clove pressed garlic
½ cup canola oil
¼ cup grapeseed oil
¼ cup olive oil

Place all ingredients in blender expect oil. Blend until well combined. With blender running, slowly pour in oil until well combined. Store in Mason jar. Shake well before serving.

Blackened Chicken Salad

3 cups tomatoes – chopped
¾ cup yellow bell pepper – diced
¼ cup red onion – finely chopped
3 tablespoons cider vinegar
1 tablespoon sugar
¼ teaspoon salt
¼ teaspoon black pepper
¼ cup lemon juice
¼ cup Dijon mustard
3 tablespoons water
1 tablespoon honey
4 chicken breasts – boned, skinless
3 tablespoons Spicy Seasoning (see recipe)
cooking spray
1 pound sugar snap peas – trimmed
8 cups torn lettuce leaf

Combine first 7 ingredients in a bowl; cover and chill.

Combine lemon juice, mustard, water, and honey; cover and chill.

Rub chicken evenly with Spicy Seasoning. Coat a large heavy skillet with cooking spray, and place over medium-high heat until hot. Add chicken and cook 7 minutes on each side or until chicken is done. Remove chicken from pan and cool. Chicken can be cooked on an outside grill.

Cut chicken across grain into thin slices.

Steam peas, covered, 2 minutes. Rinse with cold water and drain. Combine peas and lettuce in a large bowl; drizzle lemon juice mixture over lettuce mixture and toss to coat. Place about 2 cups lettuce mixture in each of 4 salad bowls. Top each with 1 sliced chicken breast and about 1 cup tomato mixture.

Soups, Salads, & Dressings

∙∙

Chicken Couscous Salad

1 14 ounce can chicken broth
5 ounces couscous
4 chicken breasts – boned, skinless
1 cup cherry tomato – diced
½ cup green onion – chopped
1 8¾ ounce can garbanzo beans – drained
1 red pepper – diced
½ cup currants
½ cup canned apricots – drained and chopped
1 7 ounce can corn – drained
1 cup jicama – peeled and diced
¼ cup fresh parsley – chopped
6 tablespoons fresh lemon juice
5 tablespoons olive oil
1 teaspoon hot pepper sauce
salt and pepper – to taste

Bring broth to a boil, add couscous. Mix thoroughly with fork or spoon. Cover and remove from the heat and let stand for about 5 minutes. Uncover and cool, stirring occasionally.

Shred or dice chicken and set aside.

In a large bowl combine next 9 items with chicken and couscous.

In a smaller bowl combine lemon juice, olive oil, hot sauce, salt, and pepper. Whisk these ingredients until well combined. Then pour over couscous, stirring to distribute the dressing.

Raspberry Vinaigrette

⅓ cup seedless raspberry jam
½ cup red wine vinegar
¼ cup extra virgin olive oil
¼ teaspoon salt
1 tablespoon pecans – finely chopped
¼ teaspoon vanilla
⅛ teaspoon freshly ground black pepper

Combine all ingredients in blender. Pour into a Mason jar with tight fighting lid. Shake well before serving.

Italian Dressing

⅛ cup red wine vinegar
½ teaspoon dried basil
¼ cup onion – finely chopped
1 tablespoon sugar
1 teaspoon dry mustard
¼ teaspoon salt
½ teaspoon dried oregano
¼ teaspoon pepper
1 clove garlic – minced
1 tablespoon red bell pepper – minced
1 tablespoon red pepper jelly (optional)
½ cup olive oil

Place all ingredients, except oil in blender. Combine until smooth. Then slowly add the olive oil. Store in a Mason jar with a tight lid. Shake before using.

Soups, Salads, & Dressings

Chinese Chicken Salad

1 tablespoon canola oil
1 clove garlic – minced
2 tablespoons soy sauce
¼ tablespoon ground ginger
4 chicken breasts – boned, skinless
2 cups lettuce – shredded
2 cups carrot – julienned
2 cups cucumber – julienned
½ cup green onion – sliced
1 cup bean sprouts
1 cup pea pods
1 cup jicama – peeled and julienned
1 7 ounce can waterchestnuts – drained
¾ cup almond slivers – toasted
3 tablespoons sesame seeds – toasted
4 tablespoons sugar
2 tablespoons vinegar
2 teaspoons salt
½ teaspoon pepper
½ cup canola oil
2 tablespoons soy sauce

Combine first 4 ingredients and pour into a Ziploc baggie. Add chicken breasts and marinate for at least one hour or overnight. Turning frequently. Remove the chicken, pat dry, and then place on a cookie sheet, bake in a 400° oven for 45 minutes or until juices run clear. Remove from oven to cool, then shred and set aside.

In a large bowl combine chicken, lettuce, carrots, cucumbers, green onions, sprouts, almonds, pea pods, jicama, and sesame seeds.

In a small saucepan mix together sugar, vinegar, salt, and pepper. Cook over medium high heat until sugar dissolves. Cool and then add ½ cup oil and 2 tablespoons soy sauce, mixing well.

Pour dressing over salad. Serve immediately.

Chopped Veggie Salad

1 cup corn
1 cup green beans – cut into ¼" dice
1 cup wax beans – cut into ¼" dice
4 plum tomato – seeded and cut into ¼" dice
1 small red pepper – seeded and cut into ¼" dice
1 small yellow pepper – seeded and cut into ¼" dice
1 small red onion – cut ¼" dice
1 English cucumber – peeled, seeded, and cut into ¼" dice
¾ cup parsley
2 tablespoons extra virgin olive oil
2 tablespoons red wine vinegar
2 teaspoons sea salt
1 teaspoon black pepper

Blanch corn, green beans, and wax beans. Plunge immediately into an ice bath. Drain well.

Place all veggies in a medium bowl. Stir to combine. Add olive oil, vinegar, salt, and pepper. Stir to combine. Taste and adjust seasoning.

Serve at room temperature.

Lemon Vinaigrette

¼ cup lemon juice – freshly squeezed
2 tablespoons red wine vinegar
2 teaspoons sugar
½ teaspoon salt
½ teaspoon dry mustard
½ teaspoon Worcestershire sauce
¼ teaspoon pepper
1 clove garlic – minced
1 teaspoon lemon zest
½ cup olive oil

Place all ingredients, except the olive oil in a blender and blend until smooth. Slowly add the olive oil. Store in a Mason jar with a tight lid.

Shake before using.

Soups, Salads, & Dressings

Corn & Lobster Chowder

2 10 ounce uncooked lobster tails
8 cups frozen yellow corn kernels – thawed
3 cups low-salt chicken broth
8 slices bacon – chopped
2 cups onion – chopped
½ cup carrot – chopped
¾ cup celery – finely chopped
¼ teaspoon cayenne pepper
3 cups bottled clam juice
1½ cups whipping cream
2 tablespoons butter
3 tablespoons fresh chives – chopped

Cook lobster tails in boiling water until almost cooked through, about 8 minutes. Drain. Cool. Use kitchen shears and remove shell from tail. Remove lobster meat and cut into bit-size pieces.

Puree 4 cups of corn with 1¼ cups broth in food processor until smooth. You may have to do this in smaller batches depending on the size of your processor bowl.

Sauté bacon in large pot over medium heat until crisp, about 8 minutes. Drain bacon on paper towels. Discard all but 3 tablespoons of bacon grease. Add onions to pot and sauté until golden, about 10 minutes. Add remaining 4 cups corn, sauté 5 minutes. Add carrots, celery, and cayenne, sauté until vegetables soften slightly about 8 minutes. Add clam juice and 1¼ cups broth. Simmer 10 minutes. Stir in corn puree and whipping cream. Simmer for 10 minutes. Season with salt and pepper. Remove soup from heat.

Melt butter in medium nonstick skillet over medium heat. Add lobster meat and sauté until heated through, about 4 minutes. Ladle soup into bowls. Garnish with lobster pieces, bacon, and chives.

Crunchy Tuna Salad

½ small jicama – peeled and cubed
1 large celery rib – chopped
2 16 ounce cans/pouches tuna – drained
1 small cucumber – peeled, seeded, cubed
½ cup black olives – chopped
3 green onions – chopped
½ red onion – chopped
1 red pepper – chopped
2 tablespoons red wine vinegar
1 tablespoon fresh lemon juice
1 tablespoon Dijon mustard
1 clove garlic – minced
⅓ cup olive oil

In a large bowl combine first 8 ingredients. In a blender combine vinegar, lemon juice, mustard, and garlic. With motor running add oil in a stream and blend until emulsified. Pour this mixture over the tuna mixture. Mix well.

Serve on your choice of bread with lettuce and tomatoes. Or you can serve this on a bed of lettuce.

Soups, Salads, & Dressings

Butternut Soup

8 cups butternut squash – seeded,
    peeled, and diced
cooking spray
1 tablespoon butter
2 cups Granny Smith apples – cored,
    peeled, and chopped
1½ cups onion – finely chopped
½ cup celery – thinly sliced
1 bay leaf
1 clove garlic – minced
3 14½ ounce cans chicken broth
⅛ teaspoon salt
½ cup extra sharp white cheddar
    cheese – grated

Preheat oven to 400°.

Arrange squash in a single layer on a foil lined baking sheet coated with cooking spray. Bake at 400° for 45 minutes or until tender.

Melt butter in a dutch oven over medium-high heat. Add apple, onion, celery, and bay leaf. Sauté 10 minutes. Stir in garlic; cook 1 minute stirring constantly. Add squash, broth, and salt. Stir well.

Reduce heat to medium-low, simmer uncovered for 30 minutes. Discard bay leaf. Partially mash mixture with a potato masher or emulsion/hand blender until thick and chunky. Top each serving with a tablespoon of cheese.

Frog Eye Salad

1 cup ancini de pepe macaroni
½ cup sugar
1 egg – beaten
1 cup pineapple juice
1 tablespoon flour
¼ teaspoon salt
1 11 ounce can mandarin oranges – cut into
    pieces, drained
1 8 ounce can crushed pineapple – drained
1 8 ounce can pineapple chunks in
    juice – drained
5 ounces of small or mini marshmallows
1 8 ounce carton cool whip

Cook macaroni according to package directions. Drain, rinse, and set aside.

Cook sugar, egg, pineapple juice, flour, and salt over medium heat until thickened. Cool.

Combine sauce and macaroni then store in an airtight container, overnight in refrigerator.

Next morning add mandarin oranges, crushed pineapple, pineapple chucks, marshmallows, and cool whip. Mix together and chill.

Tips from Chef Val

Salad Dressings

• Use the freshest ingredients from your herbs.
• Use the freshest lemon juice to your herbs.
• Using only olive oil may over power your dressing. Instead, try using canola oil or grapeseed oil.
• Store your dressings in Mason jars in the fridge for up to 1 month.
• Remember to shake the jar of dressing before using.

Soups, Salads, & Dressings

Lentil Stew with Ham & Greens

1½ tablespoons olive oil
1 cup onion – chopped
3 cloves garlic – minced
5 cups chicken stock
1 cup dried lentils
½ cup carrots – chopped
2 bay leaves
3 cups swiss chard or spinach – chopped
1½ cups baking potato – peeled and chopped
1 cup smoked ham – chopped
1 14½ ounce can diced tomatoes – drained
1 teaspoon dried basil
½ teaspoon dried thyme
½ teaspoon black pepper
3 tablespoons fresh parsley – chopped

Heat oil in a dutch oven over medium-high heat. Add onion and garlic, sauté 5 minutes. Add broth, lentils, carrot, and bay leaves, bring to a boil. Partially cover, reduce heat, and simmer 20 minutes. Add swiss chard or spinach, potato, and ham, bring to a boil. Reduce heat, simmer 15 minutes or until potato is tender.

Stir in tomatoes, basil, thyme, and pepper, simmer 10 minutes. Discard bay leaves. Sprinkle with parsley. Serve immediately.

Waldorf Salad

½ cup yogurt, regular or nonfat
½ cup mayonnaise
⅛ cup Dijon mustard
4 cups apples, Mutsu or Crispin – chopped
1 cup celery – chopped
1 cup walnuts – roasted and diced
4 cups arugula

In a medium bowl, mix together: yogurt, mayonnaise, and Dijon mustard. In another bowl mix apples, celery, and walnuts. Then pour sauce over the apple mixture. Place apple mixture over 4 plates of arugula.

Poppyseed Dressing

¾ cup sugar
1 teaspoon dry mustard
¼ teaspoon sea salt
⅓ cup cider vinegar
½ onion – finely chopped
½ cup canola oil
¼ cup grapeseed oil
¼ cup olive oil
1 tablespoon poppyseeds

Put sugar, mustard, salt, vinegar, and onion in blender, process until onion is liquified. With blender running slowly add the oils. Add poppyseeds and process until combined. Store in Mason jar and refrigerate. Shake well before serving.

Shrimp Salad

¼ cup olive oil
6 tablespoons red wine vinegar
1 clove garlic – pressed
1 teaspoon sugar
1 teaspoon grated orange peel
1 11 ounce can mandarin oranges – drained
1 pound medium shrimp – cooked, peeled, and deveined
1 cup jicama – peeled and cut into ¼ dice
1 seedless cucumber – peeled and diced
1 15 ounce can black beans – drained and rinsed
1 cup red onion – chopped
1 8 ounce can corn – drained
1 cup sliced green olives with pimento

Whisk first 5 ingredients in small bowl.

Combine next 8 items in large bowl. Add dressing.

Cover and refrigerate. Serve with baby lettuce leaves.

Soups, Salads, & Dressings

Snap Peas, Radish, & Cucumber Salad

½ pound sugar snap peas – trimmed
1 cucumber – peeled, halved lengthwise,
   and seeded
1 bunch radishes – trimmed
¼ cup sesame seeds – toasted
1 tablespoon seasoned rice vinegar
1 teaspoon cider vinegar

Cook peas in a saucepan of boiling salted water until they turn a bright green, about 30 seconds. Drain in a colander and rinse under cold water to stop cooking.

Cut halved cucumber and radishes crosswise into ¼" thick half moon slices.

Toss peas, cucumbers, radishes, and sesame seeds with vinegars and season with salt and pepper. Serve at room temperature.

Sun-Dried Tomato Vinaigrette

1½ cups canned chopped tomatoes
½ cup sun-dried tomatoes, not in oil
2 tablespoons balsamic vinegar
1 tablespoon olive oil
¼ teaspoon salt
¼ teaspoon pepper
2 cloves garlic
¾ cup water
1½ cups V-8® vegetable juice

Combine all ingredients in a blender until well blended. You may need to add more V-8 vegetable juice if too thick. Season to taste.

Spinach, Pear, & Avocado Salad with Celery Seed Dressing

3 tablespoons fresh lemon juice
½ cup salad oil
2 tablespoons sugar
1 clove garlic – minced or pressed
½ teaspoon salt
1 teaspoon celery seed
4 cups spinach greens – washed and dried
1½ cups diced fresh pears
1½ cups avocado – peeled, seeded, and cubed

Make dressing several hours or several days ahead by combining the lemon juice, oil, sugar, garlic, salt, and celery seeds in a Mason jar. Shake to dissolve sugar and refrigerate.

When ready to serve, place greens on individual salad plates. Top with pears and avocados. Spoon dressing over.

NOTE: To prepare fruit in advance and prevent darkening, combine it with the dressing, up to one hour ahead.

Tommy's Blue Cheese Dressing

1 cup blue cheese – crumbled
1 cup sour cream
¼ cup mayonnaise
1 teaspoon garlic – finely minced
1 tablespoon red wine vinegar
salt and pepper – to taste

In a blender combine all ingredients. Process until smooth. Pour into a Mason jar and store in refrigerator.

Shake well before serving.

Soups, Salads, & Dressings

Tomato Bisque

¾ pound dry shiitake mushrooms
3 tablespoons olive oil
2 stalks celery – chopped
1 small onion – chopped
1 leek, white and light green parts only –
 chopped
1 large shallot – chopped
1 clove garlic – chopped
2 15 ounce cans diced tomatoes
2 cups chicken stock
¾ cup white wine
½ cup whipping cream
1 tablespoon fresh lemon juice
1 teaspoon dried thyme
2 small bay leaves

Soak the dried shiitake mushrooms in boiling water for 30 minutes. Run under water to remove any additional dirt. Drain. Squeeze out excess water; cut out stems. Cut into strips.

Heat 2 tablespoons oil in a large saucepan over medium heat. Add celery, onion, leek, shallot, and garlic. Cook until vegetables are translucent, stirring occasionally, about 10 minutes. Add ½ pound mushrooms and sauté 5 minutes. Add tomatoes, chicken stock, wine, cream, lemon juice, thyme, and bay leaves. Bring to a boil. Reduce heat and simmer for 30 minutes. Discard bay leaf. Puree soup with emulsion blender until smooth. Season to taste with salt and pepper.

Heat remaining 1 tablespoon oil in small skillet and over medium heat, sauté remaining ¼ pound mushrooms for 5 minutes. Ladle bisque into serving bowls and garnish with sautéed mushrooms.

Serve immediately.

Tuna & White Bean Salad with Creamy Dijon Dressing

¼ cup mayonnaise
¼ cup olive oil
3 tablespoons Dijon mustard
2 tablespoons champagne wine vinegar
1 15 ounce can small white beans –
 drained and rinsed
¼ cup jarred roasted red peppers –
 drained and chopped
¼ cup chopped red onion
2 6 ounce pouches white tuna
¼ cup kalamata olives – pitted and halved

Whisk first 4 ingredients in small bowl. Season with salt and pepper. Cover and chill.

In a large bowl add remaining ingredients. Add dressing. Toss enough to coat. Chill.

MENU IDEAS

Summer Buffet

Shrimp Salad
Chicken Couscous Salad
Chopped Veggie Salad
Waldorf Salad
Tim & Dave's Avocado
Corn Salsa
Homemade Vanilla Ice Cream
Blueberry Pie

••••••••••••••••••••••••••••••••••••••

Turkey Soup with Orzo & White Beans

2 tablespoons olive oil
2 medium onions – chopped
6 cloves garlic – minced
3 pounds turkey wings, cut at joints
  (chicken wings will work too)
9 cups low salt chicken broth
2 teaspoons dried oregano
1 28 ounce can diced tomatoes in juice
3 carrots – peeled and chopped
1 cup celery – chopped
1 cup orzo
2 15 ounce cans cannelini –
  drained and rinsed
½ cup fresh basil – thinly sliced

Heat oil in heavy large pot over medium heat. Add onions and garlic, sauté until translucent. Add turkey wings, chicken broth, and oregano. Cover and simmer over medium low heat for 1 hour.

Transfer wings to cookie sheet to cool. Remove meat from bones, discarding skin and bones. Mix meat into soup. Bring to a simmer. Add tomatoes with juice, carrots, and celery. Cover and simmer until vegetables are crisp yet tender. About 8 minutes. Add orzo, simmer for about 10 minutes, covered, until pasta is al dente, stirring often. Mix in cannelloni and basil, cook until heated, about 8 minutes. Season with salt and pepper.

Serve immediately.

Tim & Dave's Avocado Corn Salsa

2 large avocado – peeled, seeded, and
  coarsely chopped
1 cup roasted corn kernels
3 tablespoons red onion – finely diced
¼ cup cilantro – coarsely chopped
¼ cup fresh lime juice
2 tablespoons sour cream
salt and pepper

To roast corn kernels. Preheat oven to 350°. Arrange corn on a baking sheet and roast for 45 minutes.

Combine avocado, corn, onion, cilantro, lime juice, and sour cream in a mixing bowl. Mix well.

Season with salt and pepper.

Serve at room temperature.

Lemon Garlic Dressing

3 tablespoons fresh lemon juice
2 tablespoons sugar
1 clove garlic – minced or pressed
½ teaspoon salt
¼ cup canola oil
¼ cup olive oil

Place lemon juice, sugar, garlic, and salt in a blender. Combine. While the blender is still running add the oils slowly. Leave running until well combined.

Store in a Mason jar and refrigerate. Shake well before using.

Breads

Mom's Banana Bread

Breads

· ·

Blueberry Streusel Muffins

1¾ cups flour
2¾ teaspoons baking powder
¾ teaspoon salt
½ cup sugar
2 teaspoons grated lemon peel
1 large egg – lightly beaten
¾ cup milk
⅓ cup vegetable oil
1 cup fresh or frozen blueberries –
   thawed and drained
1 tablespoon flour
1 tablespoon sugar
¼ cup sugar
2½ tablespoons flour
½ teaspoon cinnamon
1½ tablespoons butter

Combine first 5 ingredients in a large bowl; make a well in the center of the mixture. Combine egg, milk, and oil, stir well. Add to dry ingredients, stirring just until moistened.

Combine blueberries, 1 tablespoon flour, and 1 tablespoon sugar, tossing gently to coat. Fold blueberry mixture into batter. Spoon batter into greased muffin pans, filling two-thirds full.

Combine ¼ cup sugar, 2½ tablespoons flour, and cinnamon; cut in butter with a pastry blender until mixture is crumbly. Sprinkle over batter. Bake at 400° for 18 minutes or until golden. Remove from pans immediately and cool on wire rack.

Cranberry Biscuits

2 cups bread flour
1 teaspoon baking powder
¼ teaspoon salt
2 tablespoons vegetable shortening
1 package dry yeast
3 tablespoons sugar
⅔ cup buttermilk – warm
2 tablespoons warm water
½ cup dried cranberries

In food processor combine the first 3 ingredients. Pulse several times until well blended. Add shortening and process until well blended.

Dissolve sugar and yeast in warm buttermilk and warm water in a small bowl. Let stand 5 minutes. With processor on, slowly add the yeast mixture through the chute. Process until the dough forms a ball.

Turn dough out onto a lightly floured surface and knead in the cranberries. Roll dough to ½" thickness. Cut with a 2" biscuit into 20 biscuits. Place on a greased cookie sheet and let rise in a warm place uncovered for 20 minutes or until puffy.

Bake at 425° for 8 minutes.

Breads

....

Cranberry Pumpkin Bread

3 cups flour
2½ teaspoons ground cinnamon
1¼ teaspoons ground ginger
¾ teaspoon ground nutmeg
¾ teaspoon ground allspice
2 teaspoons baking soda
1½ teaspoons salt
3 cups sugar
1 15 ounce can pure pumpkin
4 eggs
1 cup canola oil
½ cup freshly squeezed orange juice
1½ cups fresh cranberries – chopped

Preheat oven to 375°. Grease 2 9"x5" loaf pans.

Whisk together flour, cinnamon, ginger, nutmeg, allspice, baking soda, and salt in a medium bowl. In an electric mixing bowl, combine sugar, pumpkin, eggs, canola oil, and orange juice until well blended. Add flour to pumpkin mixture and combine until just moistened. Fold in cranberries.

Spoon batter into loaf pans, making sure not to fill each more than three quarters full. Bake for 15 minutes, then reduce heat to 350° and continue baking for 45 - 50 minutes or until cake tester inserted in middle comes out clean. Cool in pans on wire racks for 10 minutes, then remove loaves to wire racks to cool completely.

Cranberry Bread

2⅓ cups flour
1½ teaspoons baking powder
½ teaspoon baking soda
½ teaspoon salt
1 cup sugar
1 egg
3 tablespoons shortening – melted
¾ cup orange juice
1 teaspoon grated lemon peel
½ cup chopped walnuts
2 cups fresh cranberries – cut in half
1 tablespoon sugar
1 teaspoon cinnamon

Whisk together flour, baking powder, baking soda, salt, and sugar. Stir in egg, shortening, and orange juice until just blended. Add lemon peel, walnuts, and cranberries.

Spoon batter into loaf pans. Bake in 2 greased and floured 9"x5" loaf pans in a 375° oven for 40 to 50 minutes or until crack appears on top and toothpick comes out clean.

If desired sprinkle a little sugar and cinnamon on top.

Tips from Chef Val
Quick Breads
These breads make fabulous gifts. I usually double the recipe and then freeze the extra loaves. Make sure to allow the loaf to cool completely, then wrap in plastic wrap and foil. I then place these loaves in a Ziploc baggie labeled with the date and contents.

Breads

．．．．．．．．．．．．．．．．．．．．．．．．．．．．．．．．．．．．．．．

Cranberry Scones

¼ cup dried cranberries
1 tablespoon brandy
½ tablespoon orange peel – grated
2 cups flour
6 tablespoons sugar
1 tablespoon baking powder
¼ teaspoon salt
½ cup butter
½ cup buttermilk

In a small microwave safe bowl combine cranberries, brandy, and orange peel. Heat on full power for 15 to 20 seconds.

In a medium bowl, mix 2 cups of flour, 6 tablespoons of sugar, baking powder, and salt. With a pastry blender cut in ½ cup butter until lumps are no larger than ¼". Stir in currant mixture.

Add ½ cup buttermilk; stir just enough to evenly moisten dough. If dough is crumbly, sprinkle more buttermilk over mixture and stir. Pat dough into a ball and knead in bowl just until dough holds together.

Set dough on a lightly buttered 12"x15" baking sheet. Flatten into a ½" thick round. With a floured knife, cut round into quarters or eights, leaving wedges in place. Brush dough with about 2 teaspoons of buttermilk and sprinkle with about ½ teaspoon sugar.

Bake scones in a 400° oven until golden brown, 20 to 25 minutes. Transfer to a rack. Serve warm or cool. Break round into wedges.

French Bread

½ cup warm water
2 teaspoons sugar
2⅜ teaspoons dry yeast
1 pound bread flour
1 teaspoon salt
1 cup very warm water
cooking spray

Combine the warm water with sugar and yeast. Let stand until bubbly, about 5 minutes.

Measure flour and salt into food processor fitted with a bread blade. Spray two french bread pans with cooking spray.

Add the yeast mixture to the food processor. Turn on the food processor and while it is running, slowly add the cup of very warm water. As soon as the dough ball forms, turn dough out onto a floured surface. Knead briefly and divide dough in half. Form long thin loaves to fit your pans, try to keep surfaces smooth.

Using a firm, diagonal movement, slash the loaves several times with a razor blade. Cover loaves with a kitchen towel and let rise in a warm place until doubled, about 30 minutes. I usually place them in the oven with the oven lights on and the door closed, works really well.

Place a pan of hot water on the bottom shelf of oven which has been heated to 450°. Set bread on shelf directly above the water and bake for 10 minutes. Lower heat to 400° and bake another 15 minutes. Bread should be brown on top and sound hollow when tapped with knuckles. Remove immediately from pans to racks.

If serving later, reheat for 7 minutes at 350°, directly on oven shelf. For easy slicing, let loaf stand a few minutes. Turn on side and slice on the diagonal using a good serrated bread knife.

Breads

Mom's Banana Bread

½ cup canola oil
1 cup sugar
2 eggs
3 ripe banana – mashed
2 cups flour
1 teaspoon baking soda
½ teaspoon baking powder
½ teaspoon salt
3 tablespoons milk
½ teaspoon vanilla
¾ cup nuts – chopped

Combine all ingredients. Bake at 350° for 1 hour in a greased loaf pan. Transfer to a rack. Let cool, then remove from pan.

Overnight Rolls

1 cup milk – scalded and cooled
1 package dry yeast
½ cup hot water
1 teaspoon sugar
½ cup sugar
2 eggs – well beaten
½ cup olive oil
4 cups flour – unsifted
½ teaspoon salt
½ teaspoon soda

Dissolve yeast in ½ cup warm water with 1 teaspoon of sugar. Let stand until bubbly, about 5 minutes.

Stir together all ingredients until well blended. Let rise overnight in refrigerator.

Pour onto floured board and divide in half. Roll into 2" pieces or cut into 2" squares. Place in a greased pan leaving at least 1" in between pieces.

Place in a warm place to rise for 2 to 3 hours, until doubled in size. Bake at 350° for 10-12 minutes. Cool on wire racks.

Pan Rolls

1 package active dry yeast
1 teaspoon sugar
1½ cups warm water
½ cup butter or margarine – melted
2 eggs
¼ cup instant nonfat dry milk powder
1¼ teaspoons salt
6 cups flour
⅓ cup sugar

In a large mixing bowl, dissolve yeast, 1 teaspoon sugar, and ½ cup of warm water. Add butter, eggs, milk powder, salt, 3 cups of flour, remaining sugar, and water. Beat on medium speed for 3 minutes or until smooth. Stir in enough of the remaining flour to form a soft dough. Turn onto a floured surface and knead until smooth and elastic, about 8 minutes. Place in a greased bowl, turning once to grease top. Cover and let rise in a warm place until doubled in size. This should take about 1 to 1½ hours. I usually place my covered dough in the oven with the light on, this seems to provide just the right amount of warmth.

Punch down dough. Divide into 27 equal pieces, shape into balls. Place 18 balls in a greased 13"x9" baking pan and remaining balls in a greased 9" square baking pan. Cover and let rise until doubled, about 45 minutes.

Bake at 375° for 17 to 20 minutes or until golden brown. Cool on wire racks.

Breads

···

Pumpkin Banana Bread

4 cups flour
4 teaspoons baking powder
4 teaspoons ground cinnamon
2 teaspoons baking soda
2 teaspoons ground ginger
½ teaspoon salt
4 eggs
1 15-16 ounce can pumpkin
1 cup sugar
1 cup packed brown sugar
1 cup mashed very ripe bananas
¾ cup vegetable oil
1 cup chopped walnuts
⅔ cup raisins
½ cup chopped dried cherries

Combine flour, baking powder, cinnamon, baking soda, ginger, and salt in a medium bowl. Whisk to remove any lumps. In a large bowl beat eggs, pumpkin, sugars, bananas, and oil. Mix well. Combine the flour mixture and the pumpkin mixture. Stir in nuts, raisins, and dried cherries.

Pour into 2 well greased and floured 9"x5" loaf pans. Bake in a preheated 350° oven for 55 to 60 minutes or until a cake tester comes out clean. Cool for 10 minutes.

Remove to wire racks to cool completely.

Strawberry Cake Bread

3 cups flour
1 teaspoon salt
1 teaspoon baking soda
1 tablespoon cinnamon
½ teaspoon allspice
½ teaspoon nutmeg
2 cups sugar
1 10 ounce package frozen strawberries
3 eggs
1¼ cups canola oil
1¼ cups pecans – chopped

Preheat oven to 325°. Spray loaf pans with cooking spray. Thaw strawberries.

Combine flour, salt, baking soda, cinnamon, allspice, nutmeg, and sugar with a whisk to remove lumps in a medium bowl. Add strawberries, eggs, and oil to dry ingredients. Add chopped pecans and pour into 2 greased 9"x5" loaf pans. Bake at 325° for 1 hour or until tester comes out clean.

Cool 5-10 minutes in pan before removing. Remove to wire racks to cool completely.

MENU IDEAS
··········

Morning Garden Party

Strawberry Cake Bread

Blueberry Streusel Muffins

Asparagus & Ham Mini Quiches

Fruit Salad with Poppyseed Dressing

Breads

•••

Raspberry Sour Cream Loaf

⅓ cup seedless raspberry jam
3 tablespoons walnuts – chopped
   and toasted
1½ cups all-purpose flour
1 teaspoon baking powder
¼ teaspoon baking soda
⅛ teaspoon salt
¾ cup sugar
¼ cup butter – softened
2 teaspoons lemon rind – grated
1 teaspoon vanilla extract
1 large egg
1 large egg white
¾ cup fat-free sour cream
cooking spray
¼ teaspoon vanilla extract
1 teaspoon lemon extract
¼ cup powdered sugar – sifted
1½ tablespoons 2% low-fat milk

Preheat oven to 350°. Spray loaf pan with cooking spray.

Combine raspberry jam and walnuts in a small bowl.

With a wire whisk combine flour, baking powder, baking soda, and salt in a bowl. In a electric mixing bowl, combine sugar, butter, lemon rind, 1 teaspoon vanilla, egg, egg white, and sour cream at medium speed until well blended. Add flour mixture. Blend until just mixed.

Spread half of the batter into a 9"x5" loaf pan. Spoon the raspberry mixture over top, making sure not to spread to edges; leave ¼" from edge. Spread remaining batter over raspberry mixture.

Bake at 350° for 55 minutes or until toothpick comes out clean. Cool in pan 10 minutes on a wire rack. Remove to wire rack to cool completely. Combine ¼ teaspoon vanilla, lemon extract, powdered sugar, and milk in a small bowl, stirring well with a whisk. Drizzle over loaf.

Sauces,
Secrets, &
Seasonings

Easy Gravy with 40 Clove Garlic Chicken

Sauces, Secrets, & Seasonings

....

Chopping Veggies

When you need onions, garlic, peppers, shallots, or any veggie finely chopped get out your mini chopper (an extension of your blender) or if you don't have one use a food processor. Place your item in the chopper and process until finely chopped. Then store in a plastic container until needed.

I usually do this with my shallots, garlic, and onions on Sunday evening as I am preparing my Sunday meal. It saves time and you'll have everything ready for your weekly recipes.

Freezing

Most recipes without cream or milk are freezable. Make sure that the air is removed and the item is completely cooled before placing in the freezer.

For smaller, bite sized items, I freeze them individually on a cookie sheet. When they are frozen solid I place them in a Ziploc baggie until ready to use.

When you want to cook the frozen item, except for cookies, remove from the freezer the night before and place on the bottom shelf of the refrigerator. Then cook according to recipe.

For cookies, bake frozen adding about 5-10 minutes to the total baking time.

High Altitude Baking

- Increase oven temperature by 25°.
- Decrease each cup of sugar by 1 to 2 tablespoons.
- Decrease each teaspoon of baking powder by ⅛ teaspoon.
- Increase liquid by 2 tablespoons for each cup used.
- Decrease baking time by 5 minutes.

Perfect Hard-Boiled Eggs

Place eggs in a single layer without stacking in a medium saucepan. Add enough cold water to cover eggs by 1". Set pan over high heat and bring water to a boil. Remove from heat and let sit covered for 12 minutes. Drain and plunge eggs into an ice-water bath to make them easier to peel.

Peppercorn Sauce

1 tablespoon olive oil
1 shallot – finely chopped
1 clove garlic – crushed
1 teaspoon green peppercorns – drained and rinsed
1 cup Cabernet Sauvignon
1½ cups beef broth
2 tablespoons unsalted butter
salt and pepper
1 teaspoon green pepper

In a medium saucepan heat the oil and add the shallot. Cook until the shallot is golden.

Add the garlic and 1 teaspoon green peppercorns, stirring constantly so the garlic doesn't burn. Pour in the wine and cook until reduced to a thick syrup. This will take about 10 minutes. Add the beef broth and reduce by a third. Strain and whisk in the butter to finish.

Season with salt and pepper and stir in the remaining peppercorns.

NOTE: Great over steaks.

Carol's No Fat Chocolate Sauce

¾ cup sugar
⅓ cup unsweetened cocoa powder
4 teaspoons cornstarch
⅔ cup evaporated skim milk
1 teaspoon vanilla

In a small saucepan whisk together sugar and cocoa powder. In a Mason jar with a lid, combine cornstarch and evaporated milk until smooth. Then add the cornstarch mixture to the sugar-cocoa mixture. Cook and stir constantly over medium heat until sauce is thickened and bubbly.

Cook and stir the sauce for 2 minutes more. Remove from heat and stir in vanilla.

Serve warm or cool.

Easy Gravy

1 cup low-sodium chicken broth
1 teaspoon cornstarch
1 tablespoon cold water
1 tablespoon fresh flat-leaf parsley –
   chopped

In a small saucepan, bring chicken stock to a boil over high heat. Reduce heat to medium, and simmer until stock is reduced by half, about 10 minutes.

Meanwhile, in a small bowl, whisk together cornstarch and the water with a fork until smooth or you could use a Mason jar with a lid shaking to combine, then whisk into simmering stock. Raise heat and return to a boil. Boil 30 seconds. Remove from heat and stir in parsley.

Cranberry Conserve

4 cups fresh cranberries
¾ cup water
3 cups sugar
¾ cup water
1 medium orange – peeled and finely chopped
½ cup pecans or walnuts – chopped
⅓ cup raisin

Combine cranberries and ¾ cup water in a saucepan; bring to a boil. Cover and reduce heat, simmer until skins pop.

Drain cranberries and put through a food mill or pulse in food processor. Combine cranberries, sugar, and remaining ingredients in the saucepan; bring to a boil, stirring often. Reduce heat, and simmer, uncovered for 30 minutes.

Spoon hot conserve quickly into sterilized jars, filling to ¼ inch from top. Remove air bubbles and wipe jar rims clean.

Cover at once with metal lids and screw on bands. Process in boiling water bath 5 minutes.

Enchilada Sauce

1 quart chicken broth
6 tablespoons mild chile powder
¼ teaspoon garlic salt
¼ teaspoon cumin
salt and pepper
2 tablespoons cornstarch
4 tablespoons water

Bring first 5 ingredients to a boil. Mix cornstarch with 4 tablespoons of water, add to the boiling mixture. Boil for 1 minute more stirring constantly until thickened.

....

Garlic Oil

2 cups peeled garlic cloves
4 cups olive oil

Preheat oven to 350°. Place garlic cloves in a large 1 quart Mason jar. Pour olive oil over the garlic ensuring that the garlic is covered by the olive oil to at least 2 inches above the garlic. Place jar on a cookie sheet and place in oven. Leave in oven for 45 minutes or until olive oil starts to bubble. Remove from oven and cool. Drain and store in a glass jar. Process garlic to create a paste, use on crostini, in pasta, or wherever a recipe calls for roasted garlic.

Italian Tomato Sauce

2 cloves garlic – pressed
1 tablespoon olive oil
1 15 ounce can tomato sauce
1 6 ounce can tomato paste
1 14½ ounce can diced tomatoes
2 tablespoons butter
1 tablespoon parmesan cheese
1 teaspoon sugar
½ teaspoon salt
2 teaspoons dried oregano
½ teaspoon dried basil
⅛ teaspoon pepper
⅛ teaspoon dried thyme
⅛ teaspoon celery salt
⅛ teaspoon dried tarragon

In a large skillet, sauté the garlic in olive oil for 1 minute. Add the remaining ingredients. Mix well and bring to a boil. Cover and simmer about 1 hour.

Bay Seafood Seasoning Blend

1 tablespoon ground bay leaf
2½ teaspoons celery salt
1½ teaspoons dry mustard
1½ teaspoons black pepper
¾ teaspoon ground nutmeg
½ teaspoon ground cloves
½ teaspoon ground ginger
½ teaspoon ground paprika
½ teaspoon ground red pepper
¼ teaspoon ground mace
¼ teaspoon ground cardamom

Combine all ingredients. Store in an air-tight container.

NOTE: I use this when I boil shrimp or as seasoning on any type of shrimp.

Brining of Poultry & Pork

¼ cup sea salt
1 quart water

Boil 2 cups of water with ¼ cup salt, ensuring that the salt is dissolved. Cool. Combine salt water with remaining water and soak according to the chart below. Make sure that the poultry or pork is completely covered by the brine solution.

- Cut up chicken – brine for 8-12 hours
- Whole chicken – brine for 8-24 hours
- Whole turkey – brine for 24-48 hours
- Pork chops – brine for 2 hours
- Pork loin – brine for 8-24 hours

. . . .

Mixed Berry Sauce

¼ cup unsalted butter
¼ cup sugar
2 ½ pint baskets raspberries
2 ½ pint baskets blueberries
6 tablespoons black raspberry
   liqueur (Chambord)

Melt butter in medium skillet over high heat. Mix in sugar. Add raspberries and blueberries; stir until sugar dissolves and berries are heated through. This should take between 5 to 10 minutes. Remove from heat and stir in black raspberry liqueur. Store in a Mason jar and refrigerate. Serve cold or heated.

NOTE: Sauce can be used on ice cream or cheesecake.

Wallace's Marinate for Flank Steak

2 tablespoons soy sauce
1 tablespoon lemon juice
1 tablespoon brown sugar
1 teaspoon caraway seeds
1 teaspoon garlic salt
1 teaspoon ground coriander
1½ pounds flank steak

Combine first 6 ingredients. Place steak in a Ziploc baggie. Pour the marinade over the steak. Marinate 2 - 4 hours. Then cook on grill 20 minutes.

Pesto Sauce

2 tablespoons fresh basil leaves – finely chopped
2 cloves garlic
1 cup olive oil
pinch salt
½ cup pine nuts
⅓ cup parmesan cheese

Blend the basil leaves in a food processor or blender until liquid. Add the garlic and olive oil. Process for a few seconds.

Gradually add the pine nuts, parmesan cheese, and salt. Remember that the cheese has a salty taste, so don't over season.

The consistency should be thick and creamy. Serve with pasta.

NOTE: This can be frozen; in fact I pour the pesto into mini-muffin tins or half of a muffin tin and then freeze the pan. When the pesto is frozen I pop them out into Ziploc baggies and store in the freezer for up to 6 months.

Roasted Garlic

2 cups peeled garlic cloves
4 cups olive oil

Preheat oven to 350°. Place garlic cloves in a large 1 quart Mason jar. Pour olive oil over the garlic ensuring that the garlic is covered by the olive oil to at least 2 inches above the garlic. Place jar on a cookie sheet and place in oven. Leave in oven for 45 minutes or until olive oil starts to bubble. Remove from oven and cool. Drain and store in a glass jar. Process garlic in a food processor to create a paste. Use on crostini, in pasta, or wherever a recipe calls for roasted garlic.

Sauces, Secrets, & Seasonings

Red Pepper Sauce

2 cups jarred roasted red sweet
  peppers – pureed
2 tablespoons olive oil
¼ cup shallots – finely chopped
3 cloves garlic – finely minced
¼ teaspoon cayenne pepper
2 tablespoons flour
¼ cup white wine
½ cup heavy cream or half-n-half
1 teaspoon lemon juice

Heat oil over medium high heat. Add the shallots and garlic. Cook until transparent. Add the flour and cayenne pepper to thicken. Stir for 2-3 minutes. Add the white wine and cook until reduced by half. Then add the cream and cook until reduced by half. Add the pepper puree and the lemon juice.

Cook for another 5 minutes. Salt and pepper to taste. Serve immediately.

NOTE: Great over fish or pork chops. Holds in the refrigerator for one week.

Spicy Seasoning

2½ tablespoons paprika
2 tablespoons garlic powder
1 tablespoon salt
1 tablespoon onion powder
1 tablespoon dried oregano
1 tablespoon dried thyme
1 tablespoon ground cayenne pepper
1 tablespoon black pepper

Whisk together all ingredients in a small bowl. Store in an air tight container.

Sweet & Sour Sauce

½ cup brown sugar – packed
1½ tablespoons cornstarch
1½ cups pineapple juice
¼ cup red wine vinegar
2 tablespoons soy sauce

Combine all ingredients in a 1 quart saucepan. Cook over medium heat until sauce is thickened and clear, about 10 minutes. Set aside to cool.

Teriyaki Sauce

5 tablespoons soy sauce
1 teaspoon fresh ginger – minced
10 teaspoons honey
2 tablespoons sherry
2 tablespoons white wine vinegar
2 garlic clove – minced
1 teaspoon sea salt

Whisk together all ingredients. Pour over chicken, steak, seafood, or pork and let marinate overnight or not less than 4 hours.

Tips from Chef Val

Making your own Seasonings

• Buy spices in bulk and store in your freezer. Don't forget to date them and if they aren't stored in the freezer throw them away after 12 months.
• Find the recipe blend you are looking for and don't be afraid to experiment.

Lemon Curd

⅓ cup lemon juice
2 large eggs
1 large egg yolk
½ cup sugar
2 tablespoons unsalted butter – cut into ½"
  cubes and chilled
1 tablespoon heavy cream
¼ teaspoon vanilla extract
pinch of salt

Heat lemon juice in a small non-aluminum saucepan over medium heat until hot but not boiling. Whisk eggs and yolk in medium bowl, gradually whisk in sugar. Whisking constantly, slowly pour hot lemon juice into eggs. Then return mixture to the saucepan and cook over medium heat, stirring constantly with a wooden spoon. Continue cooking until mixture is thick enough to cling to the spoon. This will take about 5 minutes.

Immediately remove the pan from the heat and stir in the cold butter until well combined and all butter is melted. Add the vanilla, cream, and salt. Stir to combine.

Pour the mixture through a fine-mesh strainer into a bowl. Cover surface with plastic wrap to prevent a crust from forming and place in refrigerator until needed.

NOTE: Use on muffins, breads, and Lemon Cheesecake. Keeps in fridge for up to 1 month.

Entrees

Pecan Crusted Salmon

Entrees

....

Apricot Chicken & Rice

1½ cups long-grain white and wild rice blend
1 cup apricot preserves
¼ cup green onion – chopped
1 14½ ounce can low sodium chicken broth
4 chicken breasts – boned, skinless
2 tablespoons butter – melted

Heat oven to 350°. In 3-quart casserole stir together rice, ½ cup apricot preserves, green onions, and broth. Place chicken on top of rice mixture.

In small bowl stir together remaining preserves and melted butter. Spoon over chicken breasts.

Cover; bake for 45 minutes. Uncover; continue baking for 15 - 20 minutes or until chicken is fork tender. Serve immediately.

Chili

2½ pounds ground beef – crumbled
3 large onions – chopped
4 cloves garlic – minced
1 10 ounce can tomato paste
3 to 6 tablespoons chili powder
1 tablespoon cumin
1 tablespoon salt
¼ teaspoon pepper
1½ tablespoons cornstarch
⅓ cup water
1 16 ounce can kidney beans

Cover meat, onions, and garlic with water in large pot. Bring to a boil and reduce heat. Simmer 45-60 minutes or until meat and onions are done. Add tomato paste, chili powder, cumin, salt, and pepper. Simmer for 45 minutes. Add beans 30 minutes prior to being done.

Increase heat until mixture boils. Make a paste from cornstarch and ⅓ cup water. Add to boiling mixture to obtain desired thickness. Boil 5 additional minutes. Serve immediately.

Beef Stroganoff

¼ pound boneless round steak
½ teaspoon pepper
2 teaspoons vegetable oil
3 cups fresh mushrooms – sliced
1 medium onion – sliced
3 tablespoons flour
3 cups beef broth
3 tablespoons tomato paste
3 tablespoons dry sherry
2 teaspoons dry mustard
½ teaspoon dried oregano
½ cup nonfat sour cream

Place the meat in the freezer for 30 minutes for ease in slicing. Then slice the meat into thin strips about 2" long. Sprinkle with pepper.

Heat oil in a large skillet over medium heat. Sauté mushrooms until tender. Transfer to a plate. Sauté onion in same skillet until brown, 3 to 4 minutes. Add to the mushrooms. Add meat to skillet and brown quickly on all sides. Add to mushrooms.

Add the flour to the skillet. Gradually pour in broth, whisking constantly. Cook over medium high heat for 2 to 3 minutes or until thickened, whisking constantly. Reduce heat to low. Whisk in remaining ingredients except sour cream. Then add the mushrooms, onions, and meat. Cook for 15 minutes. Add sour cream to skillet and cook for 5 minutes or until heated through, stirring occasionally.

Serve with egg noodles.

Beef Bourguignon

1 pound beef round – cut in 2 inch cubes
2 cups red wine - Merlot
2 tablespoons olive oil
1 teaspoon salt
1 teaspoon freshly ground pepper
½ teaspoon ground thyme
1 bay leaf
3 onions
2 carrots
3 cloves garlic
1 stalk celery
7 tablespoons butter
1 tablespoon olive oil
¼ cup all-purpose flour
½ cup beef broth
1 tablespoon tomato paste
1½ cups small onions – parboiled
¼ teaspoon salt
¼ teaspoon sugar
2 ounces mushroom – sliced
1 28 ounce can tomatoes – diced

Combine wine, 2 tablespoons of olive oil, salt, pepper, thyme, and bay leaf. Slice one onion, one carrot, one clove of garlic, and celery. Add to wine mixture. Marinate beef in this mixture in a Ziploc baggie overnight. Turn occasionally. Remove meat and pat dry. Strain marinade, discard veggies, and reserve liquid. Heat 2 tablespoons of butter and olive oil in skillet. Quickly brown the meat on all sides. Remove meat to a 2 quart casserole dish.

Deglaze the skillet with ¼ cup reserved marinade and add to casserole dish. Chop remaining onions, carrot, and garlic finely. Melt ¼ cup butter in skillet and sauté the chopped garlic, onions, and carrot until lightly browned, about 8 minutes. Blend in flour and stir for 1 minute. Add marinade, broth, and tomato paste. Stir until mixture comes to a boil. Pour over meat. Cover and cook in a 350° oven for 2½ hours.

Melt 1 tablespoon of butter in skillet and sauté white onions with salt and sugar until golden. Add mushrooms and tomatoes, sauté for 2 more minutes. Add white onions, mushrooms, and tomatoes to beef. Continue to bake for 10 more minutes.

Serve immediately.

Cajun Blackened Tuna

1 tablespoon sweet paprika
1 teaspoon ground oregano
1 teaspoon garlic powder
1 teaspoon onion powder
1 teaspoon salt
½ teaspoon ground cumin
½ teaspoons freshly ground black pepper
¼ teaspoon cayenne pepper
4 tablespoons unsalted butter – softened
4 8 ounce tuna steaks

Heat oven to 400°. Whisk together paprika, oregano, garlic powder, onion powder, salt, cumin, pepper, and cayenne pepper in a small bowl. Rub butter over tuna steaks. Press tuna steaks into spice mixture; gently rub spices onto tuna.

Heat a large heavy ovenproof skillet, cast iron works really well, over high heat for 2 minutes or until skillet is really hot. Add butter. Cook tuna steaks 1 minute on each side. They will make some smoke, don't worry this is normal. Transfer skillet to oven and roast tuna 5 minutes for medium rare.

Serve immediately.

Entrees

. . . .

40 Clove Garlic Chicken

1 2½ – 3 pound broiler chicken
40 cloves garlic
½ cup dry white wine
¾ cup chicken stock
½ cup whipping cream
¼ teaspoon salt
⅛ teaspoon pepper

Preheat oven to 375°. Place chicken, breast side up, on a rack in a shallow roasting pan. Place 10 garlic cloves in cavity and arrange remaining garlic cloves around chicken.

Pour wine over chicken and bake 60 minutes or until done in a 375° oven, basting occasionally with pan juices.

Remove chicken from pan, reserving garlic and pan drippings; keep chicken warm. Remove garlic cloves from the cavity, and set aside.

Remove and discard fat drippings from pan. Add enough broth to drippings to measure ½ cup. Combine drippings mixture with whipping cream in a small saucepan. Cook over medium high heat 2 - 3 minutes, stirring occasionally.

Place garlic cloves into container of an electric blender or food processor. Add 2 tablespoons broth, process until smooth, stopping once to scrape down sides of bowl. Stir garlic mixture, salt, and pepper into hot drippings mixture. Serve sauce with chicken.

Honey Mustard Pork Tenderloin

⅓ cup honey mustard
2 tablespoons olive oil
½ teaspoon garlic powder
¼ teaspoon salt
¼ teaspoon pepper
1 12 - 16 ounce pork tenderloin

Preheat oven to 425°.

In a small bowl, combine honey mustard, olive oil, garlic powder, salt, and pepper. Spread the mixture on the tenderloin and place in a shallow roasting pan. Roast uncovered in the oven for 25-35 minutes or until the pork reaches 160°.

Serve immediately.

Entrees

....

Braised Spanish Pork Chops

5 thick pork chops
1 tablespoon oil
1 onion – sliced
2 14½ ounce cans whole tomatoes
1½ teaspoons salt
¼ teaspoon pepper
3 tablespoons flour
4 cups cooked rice

Brown chops slowly on both sides in the oil in a large skillet. Remove chops from pan. Sauté onions in same pan until limp, add chops, tomatoes, and seasonings. Cover and simmer 45-60 minutes or until tender. Remove meat.

In a Mason jar with a lid, mix flour with ½ cup cold water. Add to tomato mixture. Boil 2-3 minutes, stirring constantly.

To serve, place rice in center of platter, arrange chops around the rice and pour the tomato sauce over the chops.

Blackened Chicken Salad

3 cups chopped tomatoes
¾ cup yellow bell pepper – diced
¼ cup red onion – finely chopped
3 tablespoons cider vinegar
1 tablespoon sugar
¼ teaspoon salt
¼ teaspoon black pepper
¼ cup lemon juice
¼ cup Dijon mustard
3 tablespoons water
1 tablespoon honey
4 chicken breasts – boned, skinless
3 tablespoons Spicy Seasoning (see recipe)
cooking spray
1 pound sugar snap peas – trimmed
8 cups torn lettuce leaf

Combine first 7 ingredients in a bowl; cover and chill.

Combine lemon juice, mustard, water, and honey; cover and chill.

Rub chicken evenly with Spicy Seasoning. Coat a large heavy skillet with cooking spray, and place over medium-high heat until hot. Add chicken and cook 7 minutes on each side or until chicken is done. Remove chicken from pan, and cool. Chicken can be cooked on outside grill.

Cut chicken across grain into thin slices.

Steam peas, covered, 2 minutes. Rinse with cold water, and drain. Combine peas and lettuce in a large bowl; drizzle lemon juice mixture over lettuce mixture, and toss to coat. Place about 2 cups lettuce mixture in each of 4 salad bowls. Top each with 1 sliced chicken breast and about 1 cup tomato mixture.

Serve immediately.

Entrees

·······································

Broccoli Lasagna

2 bunches broccoli – trimmed and cut
12 lasagna noodle
1 15 ounce carton ricotta cheese
¼ cup parmesan cheese
1 egg – slightly beaten
3 tablespoons fresh parsley – chopped
1 12 ounce jar roasted red sweet peppers
¼ cup butter
¼ cup flour
2 cloves garlic – minced
3 cups milk
½ teaspoon salt
½ teaspoon dried basil
¼ teaspoon pepper
2 cups monterey jack cheese – shredded
3 tablespoons parmesan cheese – grated

Preheat oven to 425°. Steam broccoli until tender yet crisp. Cook 12 lasagna noodles according to package directions. Drain noodles and rinse with cold water, lay on kitchen towels.

In a medium bowl combine: ricotta cheese, parmesan cheese, 1 slightly beaten egg, and 3 tablespoons fresh parsley. Set aside.

Drain roasted red sweet peppers and puree in blender to almost smooth. In a large skillet melt butter, stir in flour, and garlic. Cook and stir 1 minute. Gradually add 3 cups of milk and pureed peppers. Cook and stir until thickened and bubbly. Stir in salt, basil, and pepper.

Spray 3-quart rectangular baking dish with cooking spray. Spread ¾ cup of sauce in baking dish, lay noodles over sauce. Spread ⅓ of the cheese mixture over the noodles. Top with ⅓ of the broccoli. Sprinkle with ½ cup of monterey jack cheese. Repeat layers 2 more times beginning with sauce. Top with remaining noodles and sauce. Bake, covered, for 20 minutes. Uncover and sprinkle with ½ cup monterey jack cheese and 3 tablespoons parmesan cheese. Bake for another 10 minutes.

Let stand for 10 minutes before slicing.

Cheese O Ritos

1 pound can refried beans
½ teaspoon ground cumin
¼ teaspoon garlic powder
1 cup monterey jack cheese – shredded
1½ pounds ground beef
3 6 ounce cans green chili salsa
6 flour tortilla – 10" size
¾ pound colby cheese – shredded
2 large fresh tomato – peeled and
    cut in small pieces
sliced green onions
shredded lettuce
sour cream

Combine beans, cumin, garlic powder, and monterey jack cheese in microwave dish. Heat until cheese is melted. You will need to stop and stir every minute or so. Keep on eye on this.

Crumble beef into a large heated skillet. Cook over moderate heat stirring frequently, until meat loses red color. Drain off grease. Add two cans of green chili salsa. Bring to a boil and cook, uncovered, until most of the liquid evaporates.

Spread tortillas with bean mixture. Spread meat over beans, firmly pressing. Lightly roll the tortillas and place them seam sides down in a single layer in a well greased shallow baking dish (9"x13"). Pour third can of salsa over top and around sides of tortillas. Sprinkle with colby cheese, tomatoes, and onions. Bake uncovered in a 350° oven for 30 minutes or until bubbly.

Serve on plates surrounded with shredded lettuce and an additional can of heated salsa on the side. Sour cream may also be served on the side to be spooned on top of the tortillas.

Serve immediately.

Captain's Favorite

2 quarts water
12 jumbo macaroni shells
3 tablespoons butter
1 4 ounce can mushrooms – drained
1½ tablespoons flour
1 cup milk
1 cup half-n-half
¼ teaspoon salt
⅛ teaspoon white pepper
2 egg yolks – slightly beaten
2 tablespoons dry sherry
¼ teaspoon Worcestershire sauce
1 6 ounce frozen crab – thawed, drained, flaked
1 4½ ounce can shrimp – drained
2 tablespoons pimiento – chopped, drained
parmesan cheese – grated

Cook shells according to package until tender but quite firm. With a slotted spoon remove shells from water and invert on a dry cloth. Drain 5 minutes.

Melt butter in saucepan. Add mushrooms. Sauté 5 minutes. Remove mushrooms and set aside. Stir flour into butter. Cook over low heat until bubbly, stirring constantly. Continuing to stir, blend milk, half-n-half, ¼ teaspoon salt, and pepper into flour mixture and cook until mixture thickens, about 5 minutes. Remove from heat. Blend ½ cup hot sauce into beaten egg yolks. Gradually add egg yolk mixture to remaining sauce. Stir in sherry and Worcestershire sauce.

In a medium bowl, mix together crab, shrimp, sautéed mushrooms, pimiento, and ¾ cup sauce. Stuff jumbo shells with seafood mixture. Pour ½ of the remaining sauce in an 11"x7" baking dish. Arrange filled shells on sauce. Spoon a little of the sauce over each shell. Sprinkle with parmesan cheese. Place in cold oven. Set oven at 350°. Bake 20 minutes.

Serve immediately.

Jolaine's Shrimp Feta

1 large onion – chopped
½ cup olive oil
1 14½ can rotel tomatoes
2 tablespoons cilantro – chopped
1 teaspoon salt
½ teaspoon oregano
2 cloves garlic – chopped
½ cup white wine
2 pounds shrimp – peeled and deveined
½ pound feta cheese – crumbled
cooked rice or pasta

Sauté chopped onions in olive oil until transparent over medium heat. Add tomatoes, cilantro, salt, oregano, garlic, and white wine. Simmer for 40 minutes. Toss in shrimp. Cook until pink, approximately 3 minutes. Toss in feta, cook until mixed and melted.

Serve immediately over pasta or rice.

....

Chicken in Champagne & Mushroom Sauce

4 whole chicken breasts
¼ cup flour
4 tablespoons butter
salt and pepper
1 cup champagne
1 cup Sautéed Mushrooms (see recipe)
1 teaspoon dried tarragon
6 tablespoons butter
4 tablespoons grated onion
1 clove garlic – minced or pressed
6 tablespoons flour
1 cup heavy cream
2 cups chicken stock
fresh parsley – chopped

Flour chicken breasts, shake off excess flour, and brown lightly in butter. Salt and pepper and remove from pan. Add champagne to pan, scrapping all the browned bits from the bottom. Then add mushrooms, tarragon, salt, and pepper, bring to a simmer and reduce by ⅓.

In another pan, cook grated onion in 6 tablespoons butter until done, about 2 minutes. Add garlic, then flour, and cook until bubbly. Add cream and stock all at once. Continue to cook stirring with a whisk until mixture boils. Add mushroom-champagne sauce.

Add chicken to the sauce and reheat gently until chicken is done, either on top of stove or in a 325° oven for 25 minutes. Sprinkle mixture with parsley.

Serve immediately.

Chicken with Lemon & Rosemary

1 whole chicken – cut in half
4 tablespoons fresh rosemary – chopped
3 lemons
1 red onion
¾ cup olive oil

Brine chicken overnight. Remove from brine 4- 6 hours before cooking. Rinse and pat dry.

Place chicken in Ziploc baggie. Chop rosemary and juice lemons. Combine rosemary, lemon juice, and olive oil. Pour over chicken. Place lemon shells and quartered onion in bag. Turn to coat, insuring that all the chicken has come in contact with the marinade. After 4-6 hours remove chicken.

Bring chicken to room temperature. Turn grill on high for 15 minutes. Then place chicken on grill and turn heat down to medium. After 20 minutes turn chicken over. Use marinade to baste through out cooking process. Chicken should be done after 50 minutes total on the grill, but check to see that the juices run clear.

Serve immediately.

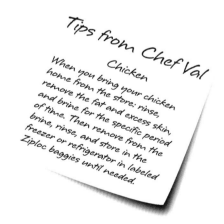

Tips from Chef Val
Chicken

When you bring your chicken home from the store: rinse, remove the fat and excess skin, and brine for the specific period of time. Then remove from the brine, rinse, and store in the freezer or refrigerator in labeled Ziploc baggies until needed.

Chef Val's Bolognese Sauce

1 cup olive oil
2 tablespoons butter
2 large onions – finely chopped
2 large carrot – finely chopped
3 stalks celery – finely chopped
6 cloves garlic – finely chopped
4 teaspoons salt
1½ teaspoons freshly ground pepper
½ pound ground veal
½ pound ground sirloin
1 pound Italian sausage
1 bay leaf
2 teaspoons dried oregano
2 teaspoons dried thyme
2 teaspoons sugar
3 28 ounce cans chopped tomatoes
1 28 ounce can pureed tomatoes
  (like tomato paste)
1 6 ounce can tomato paste
1 cup half-n-half
1 cup white or red wine

In a large stockpot, heat ½ cup olive oil over medium heat. When it is hot add the onions, carrots, and celery. Cook, stirring occasionally, until lightly browned, about 10 minutes.

While the vegetables are cooking, heat the remaining oil in a large sauté pan over high heat. When it is very hot add half the meat and cook, breaking up the clumps until browned, about 10 minutes. Transfer meat to plate with paper towel to absorb excess oil. Continue cooking remaining meat.

When vegetables are browned, push them to the side and add the garlic, briefly cook, 2 minutes, and then add 2 teaspoons salt and ¾ teaspoon pepper, cook for another 2 minutes.

Transfer meat to the pot with the cooked vegetables. Add the bay leaf, oregano, thyme, sugar, canned tomatoes, tomato puree, and tomato paste. Stir to combine. Add the milk and cook, stirring until most of the milk is evaporated, about 10 minutes. Season with the remaining 2 teaspoons of salt and ¾ teaspoon pepper. Add the wine and cook, stirring occasionally.

Bring to a boil, and then reduce heat to low, simmer for 4 to 6 hours, adding more pureed tomatoes if sauce is too thin. Adjust seasonings.

Serve over fettuccine immediately.

Chicken Paella

12 large chicken thighs – skinned
½ cup dry sherry
½ cup soy sauce
2 tablespoons fresh ginger – minced
1½ tablespoons sugar
4 cloves garlic – minced
3 cups dried shiitake mushrooms
1 pound spicy pork sausage – thinly sliced
3½ cups long-grain white rice – uncooked
1 cup green onion – thinly sliced
2 whole star anise
6 cups chicken broth
1 package frozen petite peas – thawed
1 cup fresh cilantro – chopped

Brine chicken in 2 quarts of water. Make sure to heat 2 cups of water with ¼ cup salt, ensuring salt is dissolved. Cover chicken when brine is cooled and place in refrigerator overnight.

Combine sherry, soy sauce, fresh ginger, sugar, and garlic. Mix well. Remove ½ cup for marinating the mushrooms.

Rinse chicken and place in a Ziploc baggie. Add marinade. Place chicken with marinate in the fridge overnight. Turn occasionally.

Rinse mushrooms. Soak mushrooms in 3 cups hot water for 30 minutes. Then rub mushrooms under running water to dislodge any remaining grit. Lay mushrooms on paper towels to dry. Reserve soaking water for use later. Cut stems off mushrooms and slice mushrooms thinly. Place in a small bowl, pour ½ cup reserved marinade over mushrooms. Let stand for 30 minutes.

Drain chicken and discard marinade. Place thighs on a baking sheet and bake in a 450° oven for 20 minutes. When done remove and let stand, reserving pan drippings.

In a paella pan or a 6 quart casserole dish, cook sausage slices until browned. Remove sausage from pan leaving 2 tablespoons of fat. Add rice, green onions, and star anise. Stir over medium heat until rice turns opaque. This should take about 10 minutes.

Take the water you soaked the mushrooms in and pour carefully into a liquid measuring cup, make sure to leave the sediment behind. Then add enough chicken broth to the mushroom liquid to total 6½ cups. Add to the rice mixture along with the marinaded mushrooms. Bring to a boil over medium high heat.

Cover paella pan tightly with a lid or foil. Bake at 350° for 20 minutes. Stir in sausage, peas, and drippings from the chicken into the rice. Lay the chicken thighs on top of the rice. Cover tightly and continue to bake until chicken is hot and rice is tender to bite, 20 minutes more.

Garnish with cilantro. Serve immediately.

Menu Ideas

Italian Dinner Party

Tomato Pesto with Sliced Bread

Brie & Garlic Crostini

Arugula & Orange Salad
with Lemon Vinaigrette

Chef Val's Bolognese Sauce
& Fettuccine

Lemon Tart

· ·

Chicken Enchiladas

10 6" corn tortillas
3 tablespoons canola oil
6 chicken thighs – cooked and shredded
    or 4 chicken breasts – boned, skinless,
    cooked, and shredded
4 cups mexican cheese mix (including
    asadero, monterey jack) – shredded
1 cup sour cream
1 teaspoon cumin
1 teaspoon chile powder
¼ teaspoon salt
¼ teaspoon black pepper
1½ cups Enchilada Sauce (see recipe)
⅓ cup green onions – sliced
½ cup black olives – sliced

In fry pan, heat the oil, and then dip the tortillas one at a time to soften. Drain on paper towels and continue frying the tortillas.

Combine chicken, 2 cups of the shredded cheese, sour cream, and seasonings. Mix well.

Pour ⅓ of the Enchilada Sauce on the bottom of baking dish.

Place three tablespoons chicken mixture on tortilla off center. Roll tortillas tightly, then place seam side down in the casserole dish. Continue until all of the chicken mixture is used. Then pour the remaining sauce over the tortillas, top with the remaining cheese.

Bake at 350° for 20 minutes. Top with olives and green onions. Serve immediately.

Crab Quiche

1 baked Pie Crust (see recipe)
3 tablespoons green onions – finely chopped
1 tablespoon butter
3 eggs
½ pound cooked crabmeat
1 cup half-n-half
3 tablespoons vermouth
1 tablespoon tomato paste
1 teaspoon salt
¼ teaspoon pepper
½ cup swiss cheese – shredded

In a small skillet, cook onion in hot butter until tender. Remove from heat. In a medium bowl beat eggs slightly with a fork. Stir in crabmeat, half-n-half, vermouth, tomato paste, salt, and pepper. Stir in onion mixture. Pour egg mixture into pastry shell. Sprinkle with shredded cheese. Bake at 375° for 30 minutes or until a knife inserted near the center comes out clean. Let the quiche stand for 10 minutes before serving.

Entrees

····································

Jolaine's Chicken Vesuvio

4 tablespoons butter
2 teaspoons capers
2½ teaspoons garlic – chopped
2 teaspoons lemon juice
½ teaspoon dried rosemary
½ teaspoon parsley – chopped
½ teaspoon dried oregano
½ teaspoon salt and pepper
½ teaspoon Tabasco sauce
1 tablespoon olive oil
2 3 ounce chicken breasts – boned, skinless,
   and cut into strips
½ cup chicken broth
½ cup white wine
3 tablespoons sherry
1 egg yolk
angel hair pasta – cooked al dente
4 plum tomatoes cut into wedges
10 sugar snap peas – blanched
2 tablespoons asiago cheese – grated

In a small saucepan melt the butter. Next add the capers, garlic, lemon juice, rosemary, parsley, oregano, salt, pepper, and the Tabasco sauce. Combine to make Vesuvio Butter.

Sauté the chicken strips in the olive oil until browned on both sides. Remove chicken from pan. Add the chicken broth, wine, and sherry; let mixture cook until reduced in volume by one third. Whisk in 2 more tablespoons of butter. Remove from the heat and whisk in the egg yolk and continue stirring until sauce thickens.

Combine chicken with the wine mixture and Vesuvio Butter, toss with the hot pasta. Garnish with plum tomatoes and sugar snap peas. Top with asiago cheese. Serve immediately.

Fried Catfish

3 pounds fresh catfish filets
1 quart buttermilk
1 cup flour
2 cups yellow cornmeal
3 tablespoons Spicy Seasoning (see recipe)
5-8 cups of canola oil
salt and pepper

Place catfish in a Ziploc baggie and pour buttermilk over. Seal and place in refrigerator overnight. Remove from refrigerator and pat dry.

In a large dutch oven pour enough oil to completely cover the catfish filets. Heat the oil to 365°.

Combine flour, cornmeal, and Spicy Seasoning in a shallow pan. Dredge the catfish filets in the flour mixture, coating the catfish well. Place on a wax paper lined cookie sheet. Continue dredging until all the catfish are floured. Place the cookie sheet in the refrigerator until the oil has reached 365°.

Fry the catfish filets in hot oil over medium heat for 5 minutes, turning once. Drain the filets on a paper towel and season with salt and pepper.

MENU IDEAS
············

Mexican Dinner

Best Margaritas

Chicken Enchiladas with
Enchiladas Sauce

Corn & Avocado Salsa

Classic Mexican Red Rice

Vanilla Ice Cream

Food Processor Pasta Dough

2 cups flour
3 large eggs
1 teaspoon oil
1 teaspoon water
1 teaspoon salt
flour for kneading

In a food processor fitted with the cutting blade, add all the ingredients until mixture forms a ball. Pour the dough out onto a well floured board and knead dough until smooth and elastic. This should take approximately 8 minutes. Should look like a baby's bottom, very smooth.

Cut dough into 4 pieces; keep the 3 pieces wrapped while working with one. Flatten the piece of dough into a rectangle and flour liberally. Then with pasta machine set on the widest setting, feed the dough through the rollers. Fold the rectangle in half and feed through the rollers on the highest setting 8 or 9 times, remembering to fold the dough in half each time. You might need to dust the dough with flour to keep it from sticking.

Turn the dial down to the next setting and feed the dough through the rollers. Do this once on each setting and without folding, until the desired setting is reached. Arrange dough on a dry kitchen towel while rolling out the remaining dough in the same manner as before.

Suggested rolling thickness setting (please check the instructions that came with your machine):

1 & 2	Kneading dough
3	Thick egg noodles
4	Egg noodles
5	Lasagna noodles, fettuccine, linguine, ravioli
6 & 7	Lasagna noodles, tortellini, thin fettuccine
8	Very thin angel-hair, very fine linguine

Chili Mac

1 pound elbow macaroni or other
  medium pasta shape
1 pound lean ground beef
3 tablespoons olive oil
1 28 ounce can tomatoes with juice
1 quart tomato juice
2 cups onions – chopped
3 cloves garlic – minced
1 teaspoon salt
1 tablespoon chili powder
1 teaspoon ground cumin
½ teaspoon dried oregano
½ teaspoon pepper
1 bay leaf
1 20 ounce can red kidney beans – drained

Cook pasta according to package directions. Drain. In a large skillet brown the beef in oil. Add undrained tomatoes, tomato juice, onions, garlic, salt, and remaining seasonings. Cover and simmer for 45 minutes. Stir in kidney beans. Cook for an additional 30 minutes. Remove bay leaf. Gradually add cooked pasta to the chili. Serve immediately.

Mom's Chicken Dijon

4 chicken breasts – boned, skinless
1 10¾ ounce can condensed cream of celery soup
⅔ cup water
1 tablespoon Dijon-style mustard
⅛ teaspoon pepper
4 cups hot cooked rice

Spay skillet with cooking spray and heat over medium high heat for 1 minute. Then add the chicken and cook for 5 minutes on each side. Set chicken aside.

Add soup, water, mustard, and pepper to skillet. Bring to a boil. Return chicken to pan. Cover and cook over low heat for 5 minutes or until chicken is done.

Serve with rice.

Entrees

· ·

Crab Cakes

1 pound fresh lump crabmeat –
 picked over and cleaned
2½ cups fresh bread crumbs
1 egg – lightly beaten
1 tablespoon green onions – chopped
1 teaspoon Worcestershire sauce
1 tablespoon fresh parsley – chopped
3 tablespoons mayonnaise
salt and pepper
Tabasco sauce
1 stick clarified butter
lemon wedges

Mix together crab and ¾ cup of the bread crumbs with egg, green onions, Worcestershire sauce, and parsley. When it is well combined, stir in the mayonnaise. Taste for seasoning, add salt and pepper, then taste, adjust if needed. Add Tabasco if desired.

Form mixture into cakes about 4½" in diameter and about ¾" thick or make hors d'oeuvre-sized cakes 2" in diameter and ½" thick. Coat the cakes with remaining bread crumbs, place on cookie sheet between sheets of wax paper, and chill at least 1 hour.

When ready to cook, heat clarified butter in frying pan over medium high heat. When butter is hot, carefully add cakes to pan. Do not overcrowd. Fry cakes 2-3 minutes a side, until golden brown.

Serve with lemon wedges.

Creamy Clam Sauce

½ cup butter
6 tablespoons flour
1 quart half-n-half
4 egg yolks – slightly beaten
1 teaspoon salt
2 tablespoons lemon juice
2 tablespoons white wine
2 10 ounce cans minced clams – drained
1 8 ounce box fettuccine – cooked

Melt butter in a 2 quart saucepan. Stir in flour. Cook until bubbly. Add half-n-half. Cook until thickened, stirring constantly. Reduce heat and cook 2 minutes longer. Gradually stir ½ cup hot mixture into beaten egg yolks. Stir egg mixture into hot sauce. Blend in salt, lemon juice, wine, and clams. Simmer until clams are heated.

Serve with fettuccine.

NOTE: You can substitute ¾ pound of fresh crab for the clams. I won't recommend freezing this dish, as the milk will separate.

Tips from Chef Val

When making white sauces it is always best to warm the cream or milk prior to adding it to the roux mixture. Then make sure to add a little of the hot mixture to the eggs, to temper the eggs. This will prevent your eggs from scrambling.

Entrees

· ·

Jambalaya

8 ounces Hillshire Farms Turkey Sausage
1 pound chicken breasts – boned, skinless
1 cup onions – chopped
¾ cup red pepper – chopped
¾ cup green pepper – chopped
1 15 ounce can diced tomatoes
1¼ cups tomato juice
3 tablespoons olive oil
2 teaspoons garlic – minced, divided
½ teaspoon salt
½ teaspoon ground pepper
½ teaspoon cayenne pepper
½ teaspoon onion powder
¼ teaspoon oregano
¼ teaspoon thyme
1 bay leaf
1 cup chicken stock
1¾ cups instant brown rice – uncooked
1 8 ounce frozen small shrimp
½ cup fresh parsley – chopped

Cut sausage and chicken into bite size pieces. Pour 1 tablespoon of olive oil in large skillet over medium high heat. Once pan is hot add sausage. When brown remove and set aside.

Add onions, red and green peppers, and 1 teaspoon garlic, sauté for 10 to 15 minutes or until vegetables are soft. Remove from pan and set aside.

Add 2 tablespoons of olive oil to the skillet over medium high heat. Add the chicken when the pan is hot. Sauté until the chicken is browned nicely. Add the tomatoes, tomato juice, 1 teaspoon garlic, salt, pepper, cayenne pepper, onion powder, oregano, thyme, bay leaf, and chicken stock. Bring to a boil, and then add the brown rice. Return to a boil, reduce heat, cover and cook for 15 minutes.

Add the sausage, peppers, onions, and shrimp. Garnish with parsley.

Serve immediately.

NOTE: This is especially good the next day. Additionally, this freezes very well, just remove from the freezer the night before. Then heat on stove over medium heat for 15 to 20 minutes.

Filets Mignons with Mustard-Caper Sauce

4 tablespoons butter
2 beef tenderloin steaks – 1½" thick
½ cup dry vermouth
2 tablespoons green onion – chopped
½ cup water
½ cup heavy or whipping cream
2 tablespoons capers
2½ teaspoons prepared mustard
   (like Dijon or French's)
¾ teaspoon salt
½ teaspoon ground black pepper
1 beef bouillon cube
watercress – garnish

In 12" skillet over medium-high heat, melt butter, then cook steaks until underside is browned, about 4 minutes; turn and cook about 5 minutes longer for rare. Remove steaks to warm platter and keep warm.

Reduce heat to medium. To drippings in skillet add vermouth and green onions; cook about 2 minutes, stirring to loosen brown bits on bottom of skillet. Stir in water, heavy cream, capers, prepared mustard, salt, ground black pepper, and bouillon cube; heat sauce to boiling.

Serve steaks on a large platter garnished with watercress. Pass sauce in gravy boat.

....

Thai Coconut Shrimp

1½ cups coconut milk
2 tablespoons dry sherry
1½ teaspoons chinese chili sauce
   (very spicy, optional)
1 teaspoon red curry paste
1 tablespoon sugar
¼ tablespoon salt
2 tablespoons canola oil
2 tablespoons butter
2 pounds medium shrimp – peeled
   and deveined
1 tablespoon garlic – minced
½ tablespoon fresh ginger – peeled
   and minced
½ tablespoon shallots – minced
⅓ cup fresh basil leaves – chopped
⅓ cup fresh mint leaves – chopped
⅓ cup green onion – chopped
1½ tablespoons cornstarch
1½ tablespoons water
1½ tablespoons fresh lime juice
lime wedges

In medium bowl, combine coconut milk, sherry, chili sauce, red curry paste, sugar, and salt. Set aside.

Preheat skillet over high heat. Add oil and butter. Stir fry shrimp, garlic, ginger, and shallots until shrimp are pink, about 8 minutes. Add basil, mint, and green onions and stir-fry 15 seconds. Add reserved coconut milk mixture and bring to a boil. Combine cornstarch and water then add to the shrimp mixture. Cook until thickened and stir in lime juice.

Serve shrimp mixture over brown rice. Garnish with lime wedges.

Margarita Chicken

½ cup liquid nonalcoholic margarita mix
3 tablespoons lime juice
1 clove garlic – finely chopped
6 pieces chicken
1 teaspoon salt

Combine margarita mix, lime juice, and garlic in a resealable Ziploc baggie. Add chicken; seal bag and turn to coat with marinade. Refrigerate, turning bag occasionally, for at least 4 hours, no longer than 24 hours.

Remove chicken from marinade. Reserve marinade.

Turn grill on to medium. Place chicken on grill and baste with marinade; sprinkle with ½ teaspoon salt. Cover and grill on medium for 15 minutes. Turn chicken and baste with marinade, sprinkle with ½ teaspoon salt. Cover and grill 20 minutes more or until juice of chicken is no longer pink.

Serve immediately.

Harbour Family Ravioli

1 pound butter
14 cloves garlic
3½ pound rump roast
5 whole medium onions
3 heads of garlic – separated
1½ tablespoons salt
5 large russet potatoes – whole
2 stalks celery – whole
pepper
5 quarts water
1 cup freshly grated parmesan
6 eggs – lightly beaten
salt and pepper
1 Food Processor Pasta Dough (see recipe)
½ cup freshly grated parmesan cheese

In saucepan combine butter and 7 cloves of garlic, bring to a simmer. Continue simmering, as this allows the flavor to really develop. You can make this ahead of time and leave it on the stove throughout the whole cooking process.

Place roast, onions, 7 cloves of garlic, salt, potato, celery, pepper, and water in a large pot. Cover. Simmer until beef is tender 3-5 hours. Leave all vegetables whole. Do not cut or dice them.

To prepare mixture take potatoes out and mash separately while hot. Let meat and onions cool a bit. With your food processor fitted with the blade, place all ingredients, but the parmesan and potatoes into the processor and process until mixture is pureed. Remove the meat mixture from processor bowl to a large bowl and mix in parmesan and mashed potatoes. Add eggs and taste for salt and pepper seasoning if needed. Set aside.

Process dough with a pasta machine, following your machines directions for ravioli dough. Place a teaspoon of the meat mixture in a 3" square of dough. Brush the edges with water and then cover with another 3" square of dough.

Pinch edges together and crimp. Continue until all pasta and meat mixture are used.

Boil water and salt liberally. Cook ravioli for 15 minutes without lid. Lift out carefully and place on a serving plate. Cover with garlic butter sauce and sprinkle with freshly shredded parmesan cheese. Serve immediately.

Lamb Chops with Mustard Sauce

8 double thick lamb chops
salt and pepper
½ cup red wine
1 cup beef broth or chicken broth
1 tablespoon cornstarch
2 tablespoons Dijon mustard
1 tablespoon butter

Bring lamb chops to room temperature and season with salt and pepper. In a large skillet over medium high heat, brown chops. Make sure to brown on all 6 sides. This should take about 15 minutes for medium rare. Remove from pan and keep warm.

Pour red wine into pan; scrape up any browned bits with a wooden spoon. Cook wine until 2 tablespoons remain.

In a small bowl combine the broth with the cornstarch. Then pour into skillet. Bring to a boil. Cook 1 minute.

Stir in mustard and butter. Season to taste. Pour over lamb chops.

Serve immediately.

Entrees

······························

Paad Thai

¾ pound dried flat rice noodles
3 tablespoons fish sauce
2 tablespoons rice vinegar
1½ tablespoons brown sugar – firmly packed
¼ teaspoon cayenne pepper
3 tablespoons vegetable oil
3 large eggs – beaten lightly
8 cloves garlic – minced
4 shallots – minced
¾ pound medium shrimp – peeled, deveined,
 and cut into ¾" pieces
3 cups fresh bean sprouts
4 scallions – halved lengthwise and
 cut crosswise into 1" pieces.
¾ cup water
⅓ cup crushed roasted peanuts
¼ teaspoon dried hot red pepper flakes
lime wedge

Follow directions on rice noodle package.
Set aside.

In a small bowl stir together the fish sauce,
vinegar, brown sugar, and cayenne pepper.

In a wok or nonstick skillet heat 1 tablespoon
of the oil over moderate heat until it is hot but
not smoking, add the eggs, and cook them,
stirring, until they are scrambled and just
cooked through. Transfer the eggs to a bowl
and break them into pieces.

In the wok or skillet heat the remaining
tablespoon oil over moderately high heat and
stir-fry the garlic and shallots until the mixture
is golden. Add the shrimp and stir-fry the
mixture 1 to 2 minutes, or until the shrimp are
just cooked through. Add the fish sauce mixture,
noodles, 2 cups bean sprouts, scallions, and
water. Cook the mixture, stirring, for 3 to 5
minutes, or until the noodles are tender and the
excess liquid is evaporated. Add the egg, toss the
mixture well, and mound it on a platter.

Sprinkle the noodle mixture with the peanuts
and red pepper flakes and arrange remaining
cup bean sprouts around it. Garnish the dish
with the lime wedges.

Serve immediately.

Lamb Chops with Cilantro-Mint Sauce

2 tablespoons fresh ginger – minced
¼ cup fresh mint leaf – packed
¼ cup fresh cilantro leaves – packed
1 tablespoon honey
¼ cup rice vinegar
½ cup canola oil
salt and pepper – to taste
8 lamb chops, up to ¾" thick

In a food processor or blender combine first 7
ingredients and process until completely
blended and smooth.

Place the lamb chops in a Ziploc baggie and
pour ¼ cup of the marinade over the lamb
chops. Turn the lamb to coat evenly. Refrigerate
for 4 hours, turning once every hour. Set aside
the remaining marinade to use when serving.

Heat a nonstick skillet to medium high.
Remove lamb chops from the marinade and
grill for 10 minutes on the top and bottom.
Grill sides for 5-7 minutes each.

Place lamb chops on 4 plates, spoon some of
the remaining marinade over the chops and
serve immediately.

Lasagna

12 strips lasagna noodles
1 egg
1 pound small curd cottage cheese
1 pound ricotta cheese
½ cup parmesan cheese – grated
1 pound mozzarella cheese – grated
1½ pounds lean ground beef or ground
turkey breast
½ cup chopped onion
1 28 ounce can Muir Glen tomato bits
1 15 ounce can Muir Glen tomato sauce
1 15 ounce can Muir Glen roasted tomatoes
1 6 ounce tomato paste
2 tablespoons fresh parsley flakes
⅓ cup dry red wine
2 garlic cloves – minced
1 tablespoon dried oregano
1 teaspoon sugar
1 tablespoon dried thyme
¼ teaspoon dried marjoram
⅛ teaspoon black pepper
⅛ teaspoon cayenne pepper
salt – to taste

Meat Sauce: In a large skillet brown the beef and onion about 15 to 20 minutes until the pink is gone. Make sure to break up the meat as it cooks. Drain off the excess fat. Stir in the remaining 14 ingredients. Cover and simmer for 20 minutes or until slightly thickened, stirring occasionally.

Spray with cooking oil a 13"x9" baking dish; set aside. Bring water to a boil in a heavy pot. Add salt. Gradually add lasagna noodles, make sure water continues to boil. Cook noodles uncovered until tender but firm. Place noodles on a towel to dry.

In a medium bowl, beat egg. Stir in cottage cheese, ricotta cheese, and parmesan cheese, mix thoroughly. Set aside.

Place a thin layer of meat sauce in the prepared baking dish. Layer half the noodles on top of the sauce. Spread half the cheese mixture over noodles. Cover with half the remaining meat sauce. Arrange half the mozzarella cheese over the sauce. Repeat with the remaining noodles, the cheese mixture, the meat mixture, and end with the rest of the mozzarella cheese.

Place in a cold oven. Bake at 375° for 30 minutes. Remove lasagna from oven.

Let stand 10 minutes before cutting.

NOTE: I usually double this recipe and freeze one lasagna. Any extra sauce is great over any type of pasta.

Meatloaf with Glaze

1 pound ground sirloin
1 pound ground pork
½ pound ground veal
1½ cups Pepperidge Farm Herb Stuffing
  (crushed not cubes)
2 Granny Smith apples – peeled,
  cored, and chopped
3 eggs
salt to taste
2½ tablespoons horseradish sauce
1 onion – finely chopped
¾ cup ketchup
1 12 ounce can of frozen condensed
  apple juice
½ cup chicken stock
½ cup ketchup
2½ teaspoons Asian 5 Spice powder

Preheat oven to 350°.

Mix first 10 ingredients together in a large bowl. This makes a large meat loaf or two smaller ones. Place the mixture into a large loaf pan or two smaller ones, making sure that you press firmly to compact the meat.

Bake 1½ hours or until cooked through.

Mix juice, stock, and ketchup together and heat in medium saucepan. Cook down to a glaze consistency then add the 5 Spice Powder and cook for a few minutes. Half an hour before done spread the glaze over the top of the meatloaf.

When done remove from the oven and let rest 10-15 minutes before slicing.

Hoisin Pork Tenderloin

¼ cup soy sauce
¼ cup light brown sugar – packed
2 tablespoons sherry
2 tablespoons orange juice
2 tablespoons hoisin sauce
2 tablespoons fresh ginger – finely chopped
2 cloves garlic – finely chopped
2 scallion – thinly sliced
1 tablespoon dry mustard
1 teaspoon crushed red pepper flakes
2 tablespoons orange zest
2 pounds pork tenderloin

Combine first 11 ingredients in a small bowl. Whisk to combine. Place tenderloin in a plastic Ziploc baggie. Pour marinade over. Refrigerate tenderloin overnight.

Remove tenderloin from marinade, saving marinade to baste as pork cooks. Place tenderloin on medium grill and cook until internal temperature reaches 140°. Remove and let rest for 10 minutes. Then slice and serve.

MENU IDEAS

Comfort Food Dinner

Spinach, Pear, & Avocado
Salad with Celery Seed Dressing

Meatloaf

Green Bean Delight

Mashed Potatoes

Apple Pie

Pasta with Sausage

1 pound corkscrew pasta or short pasta
½ cup pine nuts
1 tablespoon olive oil
1 pound Italian sausage – casings
  removed, diced
1 pound swiss chard – stems removed and
  cut into thin strips
2 cloves garlic – minced
salt and freshly ground pepper – to taste
¾ cup raisins, seedless – plumped in boiling
  water and drained
¼ cup freshly grated parmesan cheese

In a large pot of boiling water add salt, then pasta. Cook according to package directions to al dente. When done, <u>save 1 cup of the water</u>, and then drain the pasta.

While the pasta is cooking, in a large skillet, toast the pine nuts over medium high heat (no oil necessary). Shake the pan to toast evenly. This should take about 5 minutes. You will smell the nuts when they are done. Remove from pan and cool.

Using the same skillet, heat oil over medium high heat. Add diced sausage and cook until browned. This should take about 10 minutes. Add the swiss chard, garlic, salt, and pepper. Stirring to combine and cook until the swiss chard wilts, about 4 minutes. Cover to keep warm.

Add the sausage mixture to the pasta with ½ cup of the reserved pasta water, pine nuts, raisins, and parmesan cheese. If the pasta appears too dry add another ½ cup reserved pasta water. Serve with more parmesan cheese.

Orange Roast Chicken

1 4½ pounds whole chicken
1 orange
1 cup orange juice
½ cup chicken broth
1 teaspoon salt
1 teaspoon black pepper
1 teaspoon ground ginger
¼ cup honey

Brine chicken in salted water for at least 6 hours, overnight is preferred. Preheat oven to 350°. Rinse and pat dry the chicken. Place the chicken, breast side down, in a roasting pan.

Wash the orange and place it in the cavity of the chicken. Mix together the orange juice, chicken broth, salt, pepper, and the ginger. Pour the mixture over the chicken. Roast, uncovered for 45 minutes.

Remove chicken from oven and turn it over. Using a spoon, smear the chicken with the honey. Baste the chicken with the pan juices. Return the chicken to the oven and, basting occasionally, roast 45 minutes more or until the drumstick moves easily.

Serve immediately.

....

Osso Bucco

4 lamb shanks
¼ cup olive oil
¾ cup onion – chopped
¼ cup carrot – chopped
¼ cup celery – chopped
1 cup white wine
1 14½ ounce can chop tomatoes with juice
3 cups beef stock
1 bay leaf
1 teaspoon dried thyme
2 cloves garlic
1 cup kalamata olives
3 tablespoons fresh parsley – chopped
1 large garlic clove – minced
1 teaspoon fresh lemon zest – finely grated

Bring shanks to room temperature and season well with salt and pepper. Tie shanks around thickest portion of shank, horizontally not vertically, with kitchen string. Heat ¼ cup olive oil in large sauté pan. Brown the shanks on all sides until golden.

Remove shanks; add onions, carrots, and celery, stirring until onions are pale golden, about 5 minutes. Add the wine, tomatoes, stock, bay leaf, thyme, garlic, and kalamata olives. Bring to a boil.

Place shanks in slow cooker, pour the boiled mixture over the shanks, cover, and set slow cooker on low. Leave on low for 6 - 8 hours. Remove shanks to warm plate. Stir together parsley, garlic, and lemon zest. Stir into liquid. Remove the string from the shanks and serve immediately with the sauce.

Tips from Chef Val

Gremolata is the garnish made from minced parsley, lemon peel, and garlic. It is sprinkled over the Osso Bucco and other dishes to add a fresh, awakening flavor.

Entrees

Pecan Crusted Salmon

4 salmon fillets
½ cup flour
2 tablespoons Spicy Seasoning (see recipe)
1 large egg
¼ cup 2% low fat milk
1 cup pecans – finely chopped
3 tablespoons olive oil
1 Red Pepper Sauce (see recipe)

Combine ¼ cup flour and 1 tablespoon of Spicy Seasoning in a shallow dish. In another shallow dish whisk together 1 egg and the milk. In a third dish combine the remaining ¼ cup flour, another 1 tablespoon Spicy Seasoning, and ½ cup of the pecans. You may need to add more of each to the third dish as you coat the fillets.

Dredge the salmon in the first dish. Using your hands, pat the filets to remove excess flour. Then dip the fillet in the egg-milk mixture. Then finish with the flour-pecan mixture.

Place the salmon on a wax paper lined cookie sheet. Continue with remaining fillets. Place in refrigerator for 30 minutes.

Heat olive oil in a nonstick skillet over medium high heat. Add the fillets and cook for 2 minutes per side.

Serve with Red Pepper Sauce.

Salmon Patties

2 14 ounce cans salmon
1 cup saltine cracker – crushed
1 egg
1 egg white
½ of a red pepper – diced
2 tablespoons of parsley – chopped
½ teaspoon dried dill (optional)
pepper and salt to taste
½ cup green onions – finely chopped
4 tablespoons canola oil

Drain and rinse the salmon. Remove any bones or skin. Place salmon in a medium mixing bowl and add remaining ingredients and mix thoroughly. Form into patties. Refrigerate for 30 minutes.

Pour oil into skillet and add patties, cook for 4 minutes on each side. Serve with lettuce, tomatoes, onion, on a toasted bun.

Entrees

Sticky Chicken

8 chicken thighs – boned, skinned
1 13½ ounce can coconut milk
1 tablespoon fresh ginger – minced
1 teaspoon freshly ground black pepper
1 teaspoon hot chili flakes
¾ cup rice vinegar
½ cup sugar
3 tablespoons soy sauce
1 teaspoon hot chili flakes
5 green onions – thinly sliced

Brine (see recipe) the chicken thighs for at least 4 hours, 12 is better. Remove thighs, rinse, and pat dry.

In a large bowl mix together coconut milk, ginger, pepper, and hot chili flakes. Pour into a Ziploc baggie. Add the chicken and seal the baggie. Then rotate the baggie around to marinade the chicken. Chill at least 1 hour or up to 24 hours.

Remove chicken from baggie, reserving marinade. Lay thighs flat on a lightly oiled barbecue grill over high heat. Close the lid and cook. Turn thighs as needed to brown on both sides and baste with marinade through the entire cooking time. Total cooking time should be 12 to 15 minutes. Chicken will be done when meat is no longer pink in the center of the thickest part. Remove from grill to a warm platter.

To make the glaze combine the rice vinegar, ½ cup sugar, soy sauce, and 1 teaspoon hot chili flakes in a saucepan. Bring to a boil over high heat and cook, stirring often and until mixture is reduced to ½ cup. This should take 8 to 10 minutes.

Pour the glaze evenly over the meat and garnish with sliced green onions.

Serve immediately.

Raspberry-Balsamic Chicken

1 tablespoon vegetable oil
½ cup red onion – chopped
4 chicken breasts – boned, skinless
1½ teaspoons fresh thyme – chopped
salt
⅓ cup seedless raspberry jam
2 tablespoons balsamic vinegar
freshly ground black pepper

Heat oil in nonstick skillet over medium high heat. Add the onions and sauté for 5 minutes.

Sprinkle washed and dried chicken breasts with thyme and salt. Add to skillet. Sauté chicken on medium heat for 10 minutes on one side, then turn and cover. Continue cooking chicken for 10 more minutes. Remove chicken and keep warm. Make sure that chicken is fully cooked.

Make sure your heat is at medium. Add 1 teaspoon salt, preserves, vinegar, and pepper stirring constantly until preserves are melted. Return chicken to pan and heat through. Turn chicken once to ensure both sides are coated.

Serve immediately.

MENU IDEAS
• • • • • • • • • • •

Pecan Crusted Salmon

Red Pepper Sauce

Pecan Rice

Roasted Broccoli with Sesame Seeds

Coconut Brownies

Entrees

•••

Pot Roast

2½ pounds beef chuck roast, boneless
1 tablespoon olive oil
1 medium onion – chopped
3 cloves garlic – minced
1 cup red wine
2 cups beef broth
2 tablespoons Worcestershire sauce
1 tablespoon brown sugar – packed
2 tablespoons lemon juice
1 teaspoon pepper
1 8 ounce can tomato sauce
3 bay leaves
1 teaspoon dried thyme
1 teaspoon dried oregano
2 stalks celery – diced
8 ounces mushrooms – sliced
4 large carrots – diced
6 medium red potatoes – quartered
2 tablespoons cornstarch
2 tablespoons water

Preheat oven to 350°.

Season roast with salt and pepper. Brown roast on all sides in oil in a large ovenproof dutch oven over medium heat. Transfer roast to a plate.

Add onion to kettle, stirring until golden. Add garlic and cook for 1 minute, stirring often.

Add red wine and simmer, scraping brown bits from the bottom. Stir in broth, Worcestershire sauce, brown sugar, lemon juice, pepper, tomato sauce, bay leaves, thyme, oregano, and celery. Bring to a boil.

Add roast and mushrooms. Bake covered at 350° for 2 hours. After 2 hours add carrots and quartered potatoes. Cook an additional 2 hours.

Remove roast and let rest for 10 minutes. Cover with foil to retain heat. Remove vegetables to platter. In a small bowl stir together the cornstarch and water until smooth, then add to pot to thicken.

Simmer sauce, stirring occasionally for 2 minutes.

Cut roast crosswise into ½" thick slices and arrange on a deep platter. Spoon vegetables and sauce over meat.

Hungarian Hamburger Stew

½ pound ground beef
1 medium onion – chopped
1 medium green pepper – chopped
2 teaspoons garlic – minced
4 cups hot water
2 teaspoons beef bouillon
24 ounces V-8® vegetable juice
¼ cup carrots – diced
1 cup potato – diced
1 cup celery – diced
1 cup cabbage – shredded
1 teaspoon salt
1½ teaspoons pepper
1 bay leaf
¼ teaspoon cayenne pepper
1 teaspoon dried basil
1 tablespoon paprika
1 cup orzo – uncooked
½ cup sour cream

In a large stock pot, brown the beef, green peppers, and onions. Add garlic and cook for 2 minutes. Add all remaining ingredients except the pasta and sour cream. Cook until the vegetables are tender, about 45 minutes. Add pasta during the last 10 minutes.

Take soup off heat and stir in the sour cream. Serve immediately.

NOTE: If freezing, don't add the sour cream.

Pecan Crusted Pork Chops

4 pork chops with bone in
¼ cup flour
2 tablespoons Spicy Seasoning (see recipe)
1 large egg
¼ cup 2% low fat milk
1 cup pecans – finely chopped
3 tablespoons olive oil
1 Red Pepper Sauce (see recipe)

Combine ¼ cup flour and 1 tablespoon of Spicy Seasoning in a shallow dish. In another shallow dish whisk together 1 egg and the milk. In a third dish combine the remaining ¼ cup flour, another 1 tablespoon Spicy Seasoning, and ½ cup of the pecans. You may need to add more of each to the third dish as you coat the chops.

Dredge the chop in the flour mixture. Using your hands, pat the chops to remove excess flour. Then dip the chop in the egg-milk mixture. Then finish by dipping the chop into the flour-pecan mixture.

Place the chop on a wax paper lined cookie sheet. Continue with remaining chops. Place in refrigerator for 30 minutes.

Heat olive oil in a nonstick skillet over medium high heat. Add the chops and cook for 4 minutes per side.

Serve with Red Pepper Sauce.

Shrimp Scampi

1 8 ounce package linguine
8 cloves garlic – minced
1 cup clarified butter or margarine – melted
1 cup white wine
2 pounds medium shrimp – peeled
  and deveined
¼ teaspoon sea salt
⅛ teaspoon pepper
¼ cup fresh parsley – chopped

Cook linguine according to package directions; keep warm.

Cook garlic in butter and wine in a large skillet over medium high heat, stirring constantly, until garlic is tender. Add shrimp and cook over medium heat until shrimp turns pink. Add salt and pepper.

Spoon over linguine. Sprinkle with parsley and serve immediately.

Red Wine-Braised Chicken with Couscous

2 chicken breasts – skinless
2 chicken drumsticks
2 chicken thighs
¼ teaspoon ground black pepper
2 teaspoons olive oil
2 cups Merlot
1½ teaspoons garlic – minced
1½ cups low sodium chicken broth
2 15½ ounce canned tomatoes – chopped
1 tablespoon tomato paste
½ cup kalamata olives – pitted
3 tablespoons capers – rinsed
2 cups couscous – cooked
flat leaf parsley sprigs

Sprinkle chicken with pepper. Heat oil in a large dutch oven over medium high heat. Add chicken; cook 10 minutes or until browned, turning once. Remove chicken from pan.

Increase heat to high; add wine to pan. Cook until reduced to 1 cup (about 10 minutes). Stir in garlic, chicken breasts, drumsticks, thighs, broth, tomatoes, and tomato paste. Bring to a boil. Reduce heat; simmer 5 minutes. Cover and cook 20 minutes. Turn chicken at end of 20 minutes and cook for 10 more minutes with cover on. Remove chicken from pan; keep warm.

Increase heat to medium heat; add olives and capers to pan. Cook, uncovered, 10 minutes, stirring occasionally. Return chicken to pan, turning to coat. Cover and let stand 5 minutes.

Serve with couscous. Garnish with parsley.

NOTE: If freezing, place in container. Take out night before and place in refrigerator. Remove and bring to room temperature. Place in dutch oven over medium heat for 20 minutes.

Steak with Blue Cheese Sauce

½ pound blue cheese
½ cup unsalted butter – softened
1½ cups dry white wine
4 teaspoons green peppercorns – drained
1 cup heavy cream
4 teaspoons fresh parsley – minced
4 1" steaks

In a bowl cream together with a fork the cheese and the butter until the mixture is smooth. In a saucepan boil the wine with the peppercorns until reduced to about 3 tablespoons, add the cream, and boil the liquid until reduced by half. Reduce the heat to moderately low, whisk the cheese mixture, a little at a time, into the cream mixture, then whisk in the parsley. Remove the pan from the heat and keep the sauce warm.

Broil, grill, or pan fry the steaks on moderately high heat. Turning once. Let the steak stand for 10 minutes before cutting into thin slices. Serve with the sauce.

Entrees

....

Roasted Chicken

1 whole brined chicken
4 cloves garlic – finely minced
1 teaspoon fresh thyme – finely chopped
2 tablespoons fresh rosemary –
   finely chopped
2 teaspoons salt
1 teaspoon pepper
2½ tablespoons olive oil
1½ tablespoons red wine vinegar
olive oil

In a small bowl blend the garlic, thyme, rosemary, salt, pepper, olive oil, and red wine vinegar.

Loosen skin around the body of the chicken by moving your fingers between the skin and the meat, rub the herb mixture under the loosened skin. Rub remaining mixture inside the cavity of the chicken.

Place the chicken on a rack in a roasting pan. Lightly brush the chicken with olive oil.

Bake uncovered in a 325° oven for approximately 1 hour and 45 minutes, or until the juices run clear.

Serve immediately.

Uncle Hank's Amish Chicken

4 chicken breasts or 2 chicken breasts,
   2 legs, and 2 thighs
1 10¾ ounce can condensed cream
   of mushroom soup
1 10¾ ounce can condensed cream
   of celery soup
¾ cup raw rice
1 envelope dry onion soup mix
1 cup sherry

Place soup in casserole dish. Sprinkle with rice. Place chicken on top of rice. Sprinkle onion soup mix over this, and then pour sherry over all. Cover with foil and bake in a 350° oven for 2 to 2½ hours. DO NOT PEAK IN OVEN!

Pork Chops & Pinto Beans

4 6 ounce center cut loin pork chops
2 teaspoons ground cumin – divided
½ teaspoon garlic powder
¼ teaspoon ground red pepper
¼ teaspoon salt
cooking spray
1 16 ounce can pinto beans
½ cup salsa
¼ cup barbecue sauce
2 green onions – sliced

Trim fat from chops. Sprinkle both sides of chops with 1 teaspoon cumin, garlic powder, ground red pepper, and salt.

Place chops on rack of a broiler pan coated with cooking spray. Broil chops 5½ inches from heat for 5 minutes on each side.

While chops broil, combine remaining 1 teaspoon cumin, beans, and remaining 3 ingredients in a medium saucepan. Bring to a boil; reduce heat, and simmer, uncovered 8 minutes, stirring occasionally. Serve with chops.

Menu Ideas

....

Dinner Party

Asparagus Straws

Garden Salad with
Poppyseed Dressing

Red Wine-Braised Chicken
with Couscous

Steamed Broccoli

Lemon Cheesecake

....

Roast Pork Tenderloins with Cranberry-Port Sauce

1½ pounds pork tenderloin
1½ teaspoons salt
1½ teaspoons pepper
3 tablespoons vegetable oil
3 tablespoons butter
2 cups onion – chopped
4 cloves garlic – minced
3 teaspoons orange peel – grated, divided
1½ teaspoons dried sage leaves
1 teaspoon dried thyme
2 cups chicken stock
1½ cups cranberry juice cocktail
2 cups fresh cranberries
½ cup sugar
¼ cup tawny Port
1 tablespoon cornstarch

Preheat oven to 400°.

Brush pork with 2 tablespoons oil. Rub salt and pepper over pork. Heat 1 tablespoon oil in large ovenproof skillet over high heat. Add pork and brown on all 6 sides, turning frequently. This should take about 10 minutes. Place the skillet in the oven and roast pork until a meat thermometer inserted into thickest part of pork registers 160°, about 20 minutes. Remove pork from oven, transfer to a platter, and cover with foil to keep warm until ready to serve.

Over medium heat, using the skillet you just cooked the pork in, melt the butter. Add onions, sauté until golden, about 8 minutes. Add garlic, 1½ teaspoons orange peel, sage, and thyme; stir 1 minute. Add stock and cranberry juice, simmer until mixture is reduced to 2½ cups, about 8 minutes. Strain sauce into heavy medium saucepan. Add cranberries and sugar; boil until berries pop, about 5 minutes.

Blend Port and cornstarch in small bowl. Add to sauce; boil until sauce thickens, about 1 minute. Season to taste with salt and pepper. Add remaining 1½ teaspoons orange peel and bring to a simmer, stirring frequently. Pour sauce over pork and serve immediately.

Entrees

....

Vegetarian Moussaka

1 medium eggplant
1 teaspoon salt
½ cup vegetable oil
1 pound zucchini – cut lengthwise
  in ⅛" slices
2 medium onions – sliced
1 16 ounce can whole tomatoes
⅛ teaspoon black pepper
garlic salt to taste
10 cups water
2 teaspoons salt
1 tablespoon vegetable oil
4 cups mostaccioli
¼ cup milk
1 egg
1 tablespoon grated parmesan cheese
2 tablespoons fresh parsley – minced
1 cup mozzarella cheese – shredded

Oil a baking sheet; set aside. Generously butter a 13"x9" baking dish.

Partially peel eggplant, leaving some lengthwise strips of peel. Slice crosswise ⅛" thick. Sprinkle with 1 teaspoon salt, you may need more to cover both sides. Drain in a colander 30 minutes, this allows the eggplant to sweat. Rinse with cold water to remove salt. Pat dry with paper towels. Place on prepared baking sheet. With a pastry brush, brush oil over eggplant slices. Broil until golden brown, approximately 10 minutes on each side. Remove eggplant slices.

Place lengthwise slices of zucchini on baking sheet. Repeat brushing oil onto the zucchini. Broil until golden brown, about 10 minutes. Make sure to keep an eye on the zucchini, as they tend to burn. Remove zucchini.

Pour excess oil into a small skillet. Add onions, sauté until golden; set aside. Drain tomatoes, reserve juice. Slice tomatoes. Add pepper and garlic salt to reserved juice. Set aside.

Bring water to a rapid boil in a heavy 5 quart pot. Add 2 teaspoons salt and 1 tablespoon oil. Gradually add mostaccioli, being sure water continues to boil. Cook mostaccioli uncovered until tender but firm, stirring occasionally. Drain.

Pour milk into a small bowl. Add egg and beat with a fork until mixed well but not frothy. Pour over cooked mostaccioli. Mix well.

Layer in the following order: mostaccioli mixture, parmesan cheese, broiled eggplant, sautéed onions, parley, broiled zucchini, sliced tomatoes, tomato juice mixture, and mozzarella cheese.

Place baking dish in a cold oven. Set oven at 350°. Bake 30 minutes. Let stand 10 minutes before cutting.

Stuffed Peppers

6 large green peppers
1 pound ground beef
1 small onion – chopped
1 cup cooked rice
1 16 ounce can tomato sauce
2 teaspoons salt
black pepper to taste
dash cayenne pepper

Wash peppers, cut off tops, and remove seeds and ribs. Boil peppers for 5 minutes. Remove and drain with top side down.

Salt inside of peppers lightly. Mix remaining ingredients and stuff peppers with this mixture. At this point you can freeze these, just wrap them with plastic wrap and place in a Ziploc baggie. When ready to cook, remove from the freezer night before and thaw in the refrigerator.

Place stuffed peppers in a baking dish with ½ water in the bottom. Bake at 375° for 1 hour.

Entrees

Spicy Pork Chops

1 tablespoon cayenne pepper
2 tablespoons dried oregano
2 tablespoons ground cumin
1 tablespoon ground coriander
2 teaspoons black pepper
2 teaspoons sea salt
4 pork chops
salt and pepper
4 tablespoons unsalted butter
1 cup heavy cream
1 cup salsa – drained
lime wedge

Combine first 6 ingredients.

Season both sides of the pork chops with spice mixture.

Heat butter in saucepan over medium heat. Add pork chops and cook for 8 minutes a side. Remove from pan and transfer to a warm plate. Cover with foil.

Add cream and drained salsa to saucepan. Bring to a boil. Reduce heat to low and simmer for 2 minutes, stirring constantly. Season with salt and pepper. Spoon over pork chops. Squeeze lime juice over chops and serve.

Teriyaki Salmon

5 tablespoons soy sauce
1 tablespoon fresh ginger – minced
3 tablespoons honey
2 tablespoons dry sherry
2 tablespoons red wine vinegar
2 cloves garlic – minced
4 salmon fillets

In a bowl whisk together the soy sauce, ginger, honey, sherry, vinegar, and garlic. Place the sauce in a Ziploc baggie, then add the salmon. Place in the refrigerator for 1 hour. Turn at least once during the hour.

Remove the salmon from the baggie. Pour the marinade into a small saucepan and bring to a boil, turn heat down and reduce liquid by half. Turn oven to broil. Move oven rack to top position. Transfer the salmon to a well oiled (cooking spray will do) broiler pan and cook in oven for 5 minutes. Baste with the marinade. Turn and baste. Cook for 5 minutes more. Transfer to serving dish and serve immediately.

Menu Ideas

Chinese Dinner Party

Shrimp Egg Rolls

Teriyaki Salmon

White Rice

Roasted Broccoli
with Sesame Seeds

Side Dishes

Couscous with Herbs and Lemon

Side Dishes

Apple Butter

6½ cups Granny Smith apples –
  cored, peeled, and chopped
1¼ cups apple cider
¾ cup brown sugar – packed
¾ teaspoon ground cinnamon
½ teaspoon ground cloves
½ teaspoon ground allspice
½ teaspoon ground ginger
2 tablespoons Applejack Liquor

Combine apples and cider in a large stock pot. Bring to a boil, cover, reduce heat, and simmer for 40 minutes or until tender. Place apple mixture in food processor, process until smooth.

Combine pureed apple mixture, sugar, and remaining ingredients in a pan, bring to a boil. Reduce heat and simmer uncovered for 25 minutes or until mixture is thick, stirring frequently.

Pour into ½ pint jars. Place in a water bath to sterilize. Store in a cool place for up to 6 months.

Corn & Avocado Salsa

2 large avocados – peeled, seeded,
  and coarsely chopped
1 cup roasted corn kernels
3 tablespoons red onion – finely chopped
¼ cup cilantro – coarsely chopped
¼ cup fresh lime juice
2 tablespoons sour cream

Combine avocados, corn, onion, cilantro, lime juice, and sour cream in a bowl and mix well. Season with salt and pepper.

Serve at room temperature.

Aunt Lillian's Crispy Pickles

3½ pounds pickling cucumbers
4 cups sugar
2 cups white vinegar
1 tablespoon whole mixed pickling spice
2 teaspoons salt

Place cucumbers in a deep bowl and cover them with boiling water. Let them stand overnight. The next day drain the cucumbers, cover again with boiling water, and let stand overnight. Repeat this process on the 3rd and 4th days.

On the 5th day cut cucumbers into ¼" thick slices and place in a clean deep bowl. In a 3 quart pot, combine the sugar, vinegar, pickling spices, and salt. Bring to a boil to dissolve sugar, pour over cucumbers. Cool, cover bowl, and refrigerate for 2 days. On the 7th day, prepare 5 pint size canning jars. Bring cucumbers and vinegar solution to a boil. Fill jars to within ⅛" of rim.

Tips from Chef Val
Pickling

I hit the farmers markets over the summer and purchase pickling cucumbers. Then I make Aunt Lillian's Crispy Pickles. At Christmas all my relatives get a jar. They love it because it helps us remember a very special Aunt who is no longer with us.

Spanish Rice

1 cup onion – chopped
2 cloves garlic – finely chopped
1 tablespoon butter
1 cup rice – uncooked
½ teaspoon salt
1 14½ ounce can diced tomatoes and
    green chilies
1 cup chicken broth

Sauté onion and garlic in butter until soft, about 10 minutes. Stir in rice and salt, continue cooking for 2 minutes. Add tomatoes with chilies and chicken broth.

Bring mixture to a boil, cover, reduce heat, and simmer 20-30 minutes until all liquid is absorbed. Fluff with a fork, serve immediately.

Orzo & Veggies

1 small eggplant – peeled and ¾ inch dice
1 red pepper – 1 inch dice
1 yellow pepper – 1 inch dice
1 red onion – 1 inch dice
2 cloves garlic – minced
⅓ cup olive oil
1½ teaspoons salt
½ teaspoons freshly ground black pepper
½ pound orzo
⅓ cup freshly squeezed lemon juice
⅓ cup olive oil
1 teaspoon salt
½ teaspoon freshly ground pepper
⅓ cup scallions – minced
¼ cup pine nuts – toasted
¾ pound feta cheese – ½" cubes
⅓ cup fresh basil leaf – chopped

Preheat oven to 425°. Combine the eggplant, bell peppers, onion, and garlic with the olive oil, salt, and pepper in a large bowl. Ensuring to really mix the veggies with the oil, so that they will roast evenly in the oven. Place the veggies on a baking sheet and roast for 50 minutes, until browned, turning every 10 minutes.

While the veggies are roasting cook the orzo in boiling salted water for 7 to 9 minutes. Drain and transfer to a large serving bowl.

When the veggies are done add them to the pasta, ensuring to scrape all the liquid and seasonings from the roasting pan into the pasta bowl.

For the dressing, combine the lemon juice, olive oil, salt, and pepper, then pour over the pasta and veggies. Let cool to room temperature, then add the scallions, pine nuts, feta, and basil. Check the seasonings and serve at room temperature.

Side Dishes

Cathy's Macaroni & Cheese

2 tablespoons margarine
¼ cup flour
2½ cups milk
1 teaspoon salt
¼ teaspoon pepper
8 ounces Old English Cheddar
  Cheese – grated
8 ounces elbow macaroni – cooked
paprika

Make a white sauce by mixing the margarine and flour in a saucepan over medium heat. Cook until the flour is bubbly.

Heat the milk in the microwave until hot, but not boiling. Add to the white sauce. Season with salt and pepper. Then add all but 2 tablespoons of cheese to the sauce, making sure that the cheese melts. Add the cooked macaroni. Pour into a greased casserole dish and top with the remaining 2 tablespoons of cheese and sprinkle with paprika. Bake for 25 minutes at 375°.

Couscous with Herbs & Lemon

1 medium onion – finely chopped
2 tablespoons olive oil
1 clove garlic – minced
¾ cup water
1¼ cups chicken broth
1 10 ounce box couscous
½ cup fresh parsley – finely chopped
½ cup fresh basil – finely chopped
⅓ cup fresh mint – finely chopped
1 tablespoon fresh lemon juice

In a 3 quart saucepan over medium heat, cook the onion in 1 tablespoon oil. Stirring occasionally, until golden. Add the garlic and cook for 30 seconds. Add the water and broth and bring to a boil.

Stir in couscous, then cover and remove from the heat. Let couscous stand, covered for 5 minutes, then fluff with a fork and stir in herbs, lemon juice, and remaining tablespoon oil. Season with salt and pepper to taste.

Mashed Potatoes with Olive Oil & Sun-Dried Tomatoes

2 pounds Idaho potatoes – peeled
  and halved
¼ cup olive oil
¼ cup unsalted butter
¼ cup whipping cream
¼ cup oil-packed sundried tomatoes –
  drained and minced
Salt and pepper

Boil 2 pounds of Idaho russet potatoes (peeled and cut in half) until fork pierces easily or until cooked through. Drain and dry for 10 minutes. Combine olive oil, unsalted butter, and whipping cream in saucepan and warm over medium heat. Mash potatoes and begin adding warm liquids to potatoes with wooden spoon. Add salt and pepper to taste. Stir in ¼ cup oil-packed sundried tomatoes.

Menu Ideas

Dinner Party

Spinach Dip & Chips

Garden Salad with
Honey French Dressing

40 Clove Garlic Chicken

Mashed Potatoes with
Olive Oil & Sun-Dried Tomatoes

Easy Gravy

Green Bean Delight

Chocolate Cheesecake

Glazed Carrots

1½ pounds carrots – peeled
1 cup water
2 tablespoons unsalted butter
1 tablespoon sugar
1 teaspoon kosher salt
1½ tablespoons fresh parsley – chopped

Cut carrots at diagonal. Put the carrots in a sauté pan, they should be almost in a single layer. Add enough water to cover the carrots halfway up the sides of the carrots. Add the butter, sugar, and salt. Bring to a boil over high heat. Half cover the pan with the lid, reduce the heat to medium and cook at a steady boil, shaking the pan occasionally, until the carrots are tender but not soft, 12 – 14 minutes. Uncover and continue to boil until the liquid evaporates and forms a syrup. Shake the pan and roll the pieces around to evenly glaze the carrots. Taste and add a pinch more salt if needed. Toss with the fresh parsley.

Coconut Rice Pilaf

3 tablespoons shredded coconut
1 tablespoon olive oil
1 cup long grain white rice – uncooked
1 cup chicken broth
1 cup light coconut milk
salt and pepper – to taste
2 lime slices
½ cup frozen petitis peas

In a medium nonstick saucepan, toast the coconut over medium heat, stirring constantly for 2 to 3 minutes or until lightly browned. Set aside.

In the same saucepan, heat the oil over medium-high heat. Add the rice and sauté for 5 minutes or until well coated and lightly browned. Add the broth and coconut milk then bring to a boil. Add the salt, pepper, and lime slices. Stir with a fork. Cover tightly, reduce heat to low and simmer for 15 to 20 minutes, or until the rice is tender and fluffy.

Add the peas and toasted coconut and stir to combine. Cook for 1 minute, or until the peas are just cooked through. Toss with a fork and remove lime slices.

Serve immediately.

Pecan Rice

1¼ cups long grain rice – uncooked
4 tablespoons butter
½ cup pecan – chopped
salt and pepper

Cook rice according to package instructions or rice cooker directions. Once the rice is done, melt the butter in a small skillet, then add the pecans and cook until the pecans and butter are browned. In a medium serving bowl combine the rice and pecan butter, stir to combine. Season with salt and pepper to taste.

Side Dishes

Brown Rice with Cashews & Cranberries

1 pound brown rice – uncooked
2 tablespoons canola oil
½ red onion – chopped
2 tablespoons ginger – minced
3 cloves garlic – minced
1 cup dried cranberries
1 cup roasted unsalted cashews
salt
½ cup fresh parsley – minced
3 scallions – diced

Place the rice in a large skillet and toast over high heat for 1 minute, stirring constantly to prevent burning. Add 6 cups water and bring to a strong simmer. Cover and cook for 60 minutes or until the rice is tender. Set aside.

Heat the oil in a large skillet over high heat. Add the onion and sauté for 2 minutes. Add the ginger and sauté for 1 minute, and then add the garlic and cranberries and cook for 2-4 minutes more or until heated through.

Add the rice, cashews, and salt to taste. Cook for 30 seconds, stirring constantly. Remove from the heat and stir in parsley and scallions.

Roasted Cauliflower

1 head cauliflower
5 cloves garlic – sliced
½ cup olive oil
1 lemon – juiced
¼ cup parmesan cheese – grated
4 tablespoons chives – minced

Break cauliflower into florets. Place in a casserole dish. Drizzle olive oil over all. Season with salt and pepper. Then toss sliced garlic with cauliflower. Squeeze lemon juice over all. Place in a 500° oven for 20 minutes. Garnish with grated parmesan cheese and chives. Season again with pepper.

Steamed Broccoli with Brown Butter Sauce

1½ pounds broccoli florets
sea salt and freshly ground pepper
¾ cup bread crumbs
6 tablespoons butter

In a covered pot with a vegetable steamer, place 1" of water, add the broccoli. Bring the water to a simmer over medium high heat and cover. Steam for 8 minutes or until broccoli is tender, yet crisp. Transfer to a serving bowl. Season with salt and pepper.

In a small saucepan, heat butter on medium high heat until butter turns a nutty brown color. Add the crumbs and toss with the butter. Pour the buttered crumbs onto the broccoli and toss to coat.

Menu Ideas

Garden Salad with
Balsamic-Port Dressing

Roast Pork Tenderloins with
Cranberry – Port Sauce

Brown Rice with Cashews
& Cranberries

Pumpkin Pie

Side Dishes

Roasted Broccoli with Sesame Seeds

1 pound broccoli florets
2 tablespoons olive oil
salt and pepper
2 tablespoons butter
1 teaspoon garlic – minced
½ teaspoon lemon zest – grated
2 tablespoons fresh lemon juice
2 tablespoons toasted sesame seeds

Preheat oven to 500°.

In a large bowl toss the broccoli with the oil and lightly sprinkle with salt and pepper. Arrange the broccoli in a single layer on a baking sheet and roast. Turn broccoli after 6 minutes. Cook for 12 minutes total or until tender.

In a small saucepan, melt the butter over medium heat. Add the garlic and lemon zest. Stir for 1 minute. Let cool slightly and stir in lemon juice. Place broccoli in a serving bowl; pour the lemon butter over it and toss to coat. Scatter the toasted sesame seeds over the top.

Sautéed Mushrooms

3 pounds mushrooms
6 tablespoons butter
½ cup dry vermouth
3 tablespoons onion – grated
½ teaspoon salt
¼ teaspoon pepper

Remove stems from cleaned mushrooms and slice. In a skillet melt butter and add vermouth, onion, salt, and pepper. Bring to a boil and continue cooking until almost all of the wine is boiled off. Add the mushrooms and continue to cook until the mushrooms have lost their liquid. They will look shiny.

Serve immediately or store in the refrigerator for up to 2 weeks.

Sautéed Broccoli with Shallots

½ cup balsamic vinegar
2 large shallots – finely chopped
4 tablespoons butter – room temperature
2 pounds broccoli – trimmed

Combine vinegar and shallots in heavy small saucepan. Boil over medium heat until almost all vinegar is absorbed, stirring frequently, about 6 minutes. Cool completely. Add butter, and mix until well blended.

Cook broccoli in large pot of boiling salted water until crisp-tender. Transfer to an ice bath. Drain. Rinse under cold water; drain well. Pat dry with paper towels.

Combine broccoli and balsamic-butter in large nonstick skillet. Toss over medium heat until broccoli is heated through, about 5 minutes. Season to taste with salt and pepper.

Side Dishes

Classic Mexican Red Rice

1 14½ ounce can peeled whole tomatoes
   in juice – drained
3 tablespoons white onion – chopped
2 small cloves garlic – peeled
¼ cup canola oil
1 cup medium grain white rice – uncooked
1 cup hot water
1 medium carrot – peeled, cut into ¼" dice
⅓ cup fresh or frozen peas
⅓ cup fresh or frozen corn kernels
2 Serrano chilies – halved lengthwise, seeded
1 teaspoon salt

Puree tomatoes, onion, and garlic in blender until smooth. Set tomato puree aside.

Heat oil in saucepan over medium high heat. Add rice, stir until rice is pale golden, about 1 minute. Stir in tomato puree, then 1 cup hot water, carrot, peas, corn, chilies, and salt. Bring to a boil. Reduce heat to low, cover, and cook until almost all liquid is absorbed. This should take about 20 minutes.

Uncover and cook until rice is tender and all liquid is absorbed, about 10 more minutes.

Remove from heat, cover, and let stand 5 minutes. Discard chilies. Fluff rice with fork

Basmati Rice Pilaf

½ cup onion – finely chopped
⅓ cup slivered almond
2 tablespoons butter or margarine
1 cup basmati rice – uncooked
½ cup carrot – finely chopped
⅓ cup currants
1 teaspoon orange peel – finely shredded
¼ teaspoon ground cinnamon
⅛ teaspoon red pepper – crushed
⅛ teaspoon black pepper
1 14½ ounce can chicken broth
¼ cup water

In a medium saucepan cook onion and almonds over medium heat in hot butter or margarine about 5 minutes or until onion is tender and almonds are golden. Stir in uncooked rice. Cook and stir for 4 minutes. Stir in carrots, currants, orange peel, cinnamon, black pepper, and red pepper.

Carefully stir in chicken broth and water into saucepan. Bring to boiling; reduce heat. Simmer, covered about 20 minutes or until liquid is absorbed and rice is tender.

MENU IDEAS

Dinner Party

Salmon Mousse & Crackers

Garden Salad with Lemon
Garlic Dressing

Orange Roasted Chicken

Basmati Rice Pilaf

Fresh Apple Cake

....

Wild Rice & Toasted Pecan Pilaf

1 cup pecan – chopped coarsely
2 tablespoons unsalted butter – melted
¾ teaspoon dried thyme
¼ teaspoon salt
1 large onion – halved lengthwise and
  sliced thin lengthwise
1 yellow bell pepper – julienne
¼ cup olive oil
2½ cups wild rice – uncooked
4½ cups chicken broth

Preheat the oven to 375°. In a small baking pan toss the pecans with the butter, thyme, and salt until they are well coated and toast them in the middle of the oven for 10 minutes, or until they are crisp and fragrant. You can also do this on the stovetop over medium heat, but make sure to watch the nuts as they will burn quickly.

In a ovenproof casserole dish cook the onion and the bell pepper in the oil over moderately low heat, stirring, for 5 minutes, or until they are just softened. With a slotted spoon transfer them to a bowl. Add the rice to the casserole and cook, stirring constantly, for 1 minute. Stir in the broth, bring to a boil, salt, and pepper to taste. Bake the mixture, covered, in the middle of the oven for 40 minutes. Stir in the onion mixture, bake the pilaf, covered for 30 minutes more, or until the rice is tender and the broth has been absorbed. Stir in the pecans.

Uncle Hank's Baked Beans

1 pound navy beans – uncooked
4 tablespoons oil
3 tablespoons catsup
3 tablespoons dark molasses
¾ tablespoon dry mustard
1 large onion – chopped
1 teaspoon salt and pepper
3 tablespoons brown sugar

Soak the beans overnight. Drain and place the beans in a stock pot and bring to a boil. Continue to boil until the beans feel soft but firm. Place the beans with their juice in a bean pot. Add remaining ingredients. Cook in a 350° oven uncovered for 4 to 6 hours. Add hot water as necessary.

Green Bean Delight

2 to 3 pounds fresh green beans
4 tablespoons butter – divided
3 ribs celery – cut ½" thick, cut diagonally
1 bunch green onion – cut in 1" lengths
salt and pepper

Pre-cook green beans until almost tender.

When ready to serve, melt two tablespoons butter in a skillet and cook celery for a few minutes. Add green onions and toss. Add green beans and stir until heated through. Add remaining butter and season to taste.

Desserts

Apricot Chocolate Cookies,
Lemon Cheesecake with
Lemon Curd, & Macaroons

Desserts

Aunt Lillian's Squash Pie

1½ cups milk – warmed
¾ cup sugar
1 teaspoon salt
¾ teaspoon ground ginger
¾ teaspoon ground nutmeg
½ teaspoon cinnamon
2 eggs
2½ cups winter or Hubbard squash –
   cooked, drained, and mashed
1 unbaked Pie Crust (see recipe)

Preheat oven to 450°.

Heat milk in a saucepan over medium low heat.

Whisk sugar, salt, ginger, nutmeg, and cinnamon together to remove any lumps. Beat eggs slightly. Stir the dry ingredients into the eggs and add the squash. Next add the warm milk. If filling looks too thin to you, don't be alarmed. It will thicken as it cooks.

Pour mixture into unbaked pie shell. Bake for 15 minutes, and then reduce oven to 350° and bake for an additional 30 minutes. The filling should be firm across the pie. You can make certain it is done, by tipping the pie pan slightly. If the center moves it needs a little more cooking.

Cool before serving, but don't chill as it ruins the pastry and filling.

Oatmeal Raisin Cookies

1 cup brown sugar – firmly packed
½ cup sugar
1 cup margarine or butter – softened
2 eggs
1 teaspoon vanilla
1½ cups all-purpose flour
1 teaspoon baking soda
1 teaspoon cinnamon
½ teaspoon salt
3 cups Quaker Oats – uncooked
1 cup raisins

Heat oven to 350°. Beat together sugars and margarine-butter until creamy. Might take 3 minutes. Add eggs and vanilla, beat well.

Combine flour, baking soda, cinnamon, and salt with a whisk. Add flour mixture to egg mixture, mixing well.

Stir in oats and raisins. Drop by rounded tablespoonfuls onto ungreased cookie sheet.

Bake 10 to 12 minutes or until golden brown.

Cool 1 minute on cookie sheet then remove to wire rack.

Apricot Chocolate Cookies

½ cup dried apricot – chopped
½ cup orange juice
¼ cup butter – softened
⅔ cup sugar
⅓ cup brown sugar – packed
2 large egg whites
1 teaspoon vanilla
1½ cups flour
½ cup cocoa
½ teaspoon baking soda
¼ teaspoon baking powder
¼ teaspoon salt
1 cup white chocolate chunks

Preheat the oven to 350°.

Place the apricots and orange juice in a saucepan and heat over medium high heat. Bring to a boil. Boil for 2 minutes. Remove from heat and cool.

Using your electric mixer, combine the butter and sugars until fluffy, about 3 minutes. Scrape down the bowl and beat until combined. Add the egg whites and vanilla.

In medium bowl whisk together the flour, baking soda, baking powder, and salt. Whisking removes the lumps, same as sifting.

Add the apricot mixture to the butter mixture and combine. Then add the flour mixture and the white chocolate chunks.

Drop by rounded tablespoons onto a greased cookie sheet, spacing the dough 2" apart. Bake for 10-12 minutes, until soft in the middle, but set around the edges. Transfer to a wire rack to cool.

NOTE: I sometimes double the recipe. Taking a 1 ounce scoop, I scoop out the extra dough onto a waxed lined cookie sheet. When the cookie sheet is full or I run out of dough, I place the cookie sheet in the freezer.

When the dough is frozen I remove the balls and put them in a Ziploc bag, usually 16 to a bag and then I label the baggie and re-freeze them. Then whenever I want to have some hot homemade cookies, I can go to the freezer and pop the frozen cookies into the oven. I usually add 5 to 8 minutes to the overall baking time if the cookies are frozen.

Desserts

∙∙

Refrigerator Chocolate Cookies

2 cups sugar
½ cup milk
dash salt
½ cup cocoa
½ cup margarine
4 cups rolled oats – uncooked
1 cup peanut butter
1 teaspoon vanilla

Place sugar, milk, salt, cocoa, and margarine in a heavy saucepan over medium heat. Heat until margarine is melted. Bring to a full boil. Boil for 2 minutes. Remove from the stove and add the oatmeal, peanut butter, and vanilla. Stir until blended and spoon onto wax paper. Place in refrigerator for 30 minutes.

Keep in the refrigerator for up to 1 week.

Blueberry Cake

½ cup light molasses
½ cup canola oil
1 cup sugar
1 egg
1 teaspoon salt
½ teaspoon ground cloves
½ teaspoon ground ginger
½ teaspoon ground cinnamon
2 teaspoons baking soda
2½ cups flour
1 cup boiling water
1½ cups fresh or frozen blueberries

Mix all ingredients except blueberries, stirring well after each addition. Lightly flour blueberries and gently fold into the batter. Bake in a greased 10"x10"x2" pan at 350° for 40 minutes or until tester comes out dry.

Chocolate Fudge Cake

1 cup flour
2 teaspoons baking powder
¼ teaspoon salt
¾ cup sugar
6 tablespoons cocoa – divided
½ cup skim milk
2 tablespoons canola oil
1 cup brown sugar – firmly packed
1¾ cups hot water
whipping cream

In a medium bowl, whisk together the flour, baking powder, salt, sugar, and 4 tablespoons cocoa. Mix in the milk and oil. Spread in an ungreased 8" square pan.

Mix remaining 2 tablespoons of cocoa and all the brown sugar, sprinkle over the batter. Dribble the hot water evenly onto the batter.

Bake at 350° for 45 minutes. Serve warm with whipping cream or ice cream.

The cake rises to the top while the sauce forms in the bottom.

Tips from Chef Val

Freezing Fruit

Wash your fruit, then dry, and spread in a single layer on a cookie sheet lined with wax paper. Place cookie sheet in freezer. When fruit is frozen solid, place in a Ziploc baggie.

Desserts

Best Ever Chocolate Cake

2 sticks margarine
1 cup water
4 tablespoons cocoa
2 cups flour
2 cups sugar
2 eggs
1 teaspoon soda
1 teaspoon cinnamon
½ cup buttermilk
1 Best Ever Chocolate Frosting (see recipe)

Preheat oven to 350°.

Boil first three ingredients.

Combine next 2 ingredients, whisk to remove any lumps. Then pour boiled mixture over this. Beat well using an electric mixer.

Add remaining ingredients, beat well, and pour into ungreased sheet pan or 2 8" well greased cake pans. Bake at 350° for 25 minutes. Cool on wire racks. Frost with Best Ever Chocolate Frosting.

Chocolate Curls

8 ounces semisweet chocolate
1 teaspoon vegetable shortening

Melt the chocolate and shortening slowly over low to medium heat. Stirring occasionally.

Flip two 11"x17" cookie sheets over, if they have sides, overwise use as you normally would. Then divide the chocolate between the two pans. Spread the chocolate evenly with an offset spatula. Chill until your finger makes a mark when touched.

Remove the pans from the refrigerator. Hold a sturdy bench scrapper at a 45° angle to the pan, scraping away from you, forming curls. If too soft return to refrigerator, if too cold leave at room temperature for a few minutes.

Place curls and shavings onto a parchment lined cookie sheet and refrigerate for 30 minutes. Then decorate as desired. If the curls become too soft, return to refrigerator for 15-30 minutes.

NOTE: These chocolate curls can be used on cupcakes, or as a decoration on any dessert.

Best Ever Chocolate Frosting

1 stick margarine
4 tablespoons cocoa
6 tablespoons milk
1 box powdered sugar – sifted
1 teaspoon vanilla

Combine first three ingredients in a medium saucepan and bring to a boil. Cool and add box of powdered sugar and vanilla. Beat well with an electric mixer. I usually cool the frosting prior to frosting the cake. Make sure cake is completely cooled before frosting.

. . . .

Chocolaty Peanut Butter Cookies

2 cups flour
½ cup cocoa powder
½ teaspoon baking powder
½ teaspoon baking soda
½ cup butter – at room temperature
½ cup vegetable shortening
½ cup sugar
1 cup light brown sugar
2 large eggs
1 teaspoon vanilla
1 cup semisweet chocolate chips
½ cup peanut butter
¼ cup brown sugar

Whisk together the flour, cocoa, baking powder, and baking soda. Set aside.

Using your electric mixer, beat the butter, shortening, sugar, and 1 cup of the brown sugar until light and fluffy at medium speed for 3 minutes. Add eggs one at a time. Scrapping down the sides of the bowl after each egg addition. Add vanilla and beat to combine.

Gradually add all dry ingredients, mixing on low speed. Then add the chips. Cover and chill for 1 hour.

Combine the peanut butter with ¼ cup of brown sugar. Set aside.

Using a 1 ounce cookie scoop, drop dough onto cookie sheet. Make a thumb print in the top and fill the hole with the peanut butter mixture. Top with a second heaping tablespoon of flattened dough. Carefully press the top of the cookie to the bottom cookie, making sure to cover the peanut butter filling.

Bake in a 350° oven for 12-15 minutes. Allow the cookies to cool on the cookie sheet for 5 minutes before transferring to a rack to cool completely.

Blueberry Cobbler

6 cups fresh blueberries
⅓ cup sugar
2 tablespoons cornstarch
1 teaspoon lemon rind – grated
1⅓ cups flour
2 tablespoons sugar
¾ teaspoon baking powder
¼ teaspoon salt
¼ teaspoon baking soda
5 tablespoons chilled butter – cut into
  small pieces
1 cup fat free sour cream
3 tablespoons 2% low fat milk
1 teaspoon sugar

Preheat oven to 350°.

Mix together first 4 ingredients and pour into an 11"x7" baking dish.

Combine flour, sugar, baking powder, salt, and baking soda in a large bowl. Use a whisk to remove any lumps. Cut in butter with a pastry blender. Stir in sour cream to form soft dough.

Drop dough by spoonfuls onto blueberry mixture to form 8 dumplings. Brush dumplings with milk, sprinkle with 1 teaspoon sugar.

Place baking dish on a cookie sheet. Bake at 350° for 50 to 60 minutes or until bubbly and dumplings are browned. Depending on your oven, the dumplings may brown faster than the filling cooks, if this is the case, place foil over the top and continue to bake.

Chocolate Cheesecake with Hot Fudge Sauce

2 cups crushed saltine crackers
1 cup walnuts – finely chopped
⅔ cup butter or margarine – melted
⅓ cup sugar
12 1 ounce squares semisweet chocolate
1½ cups butter
2 8 ounce packages cream cheese – softened
1½ cups sugar
6 eggs

Hot Fudge Sauce
1 12 ounce package semisweet
   chocolate chips
1 cup half-n-half
1 tablespoon butter or margarine
1 teaspoon vanilla extract

Combine first 4 ingredients, stirring well. Transfer into a lightly greased 9" springform pan. Using a dry measuring cup, evenly press crumbs into the sides and around the bottom. Bake at 350° for 8 minutes. Remove and let cool on a wire rack.

Turn oven down to 300°.

Combine chocolate squares and 1½ cups butter in a heavy saucepan. Cook over medium low heat until mixture is melted and smooth. Stir frequently. Remove from heat and let cool.

Beat cream cheese at medium speed until creamy. Add 1½ cups sugar. Beat well. Add eggs, one at a time combining well after each addition. Scrap down the sides of the bowl after each egg addition. Add cooled chocolate mixture. Pour into a prepared crust.

Bake at 300° for 1 hour and 30 minutes or until almost set. Turn oven off. Let cheesecake cool in oven 1 hour. Remove to a wire rack, let cool to room temperature.

Remove sides of pan. Serve cheesecake at room temperature with Hot Fudge Sauce, or chill until ready to serve.

Hot Fudge Sauce: Combine 12 ounce package of chips and half-n-half in a saucepan. Cook over medium heat until chocolate melts and mixture is smooth, stirring frequently. Remove from heat, stir in butter and vanilla. Serve warm.

NOTE: I have made these into tartlets using mini-muffin tins. Bake the smaller ones for 15 minutes, then check. If not done continue baking but check on them every few minutes, because you do not want to overbake the smaller ones.

Desperts

....

Chocolate Fudge

½ cup light or dark corn syrup
⅓ cup evaporated milk
3 cups semisweet chocolate chip
¾ cup confectioner's sugar
2 teaspoons vanilla
1 cup nuts (optional) – coarsely chopped

Line an 8" square pan with plastic wrap. In a 3 quart microwaveable bowl, stir together corn syrup and milk until smooth. Microwave on high 3 minutes. Stir in chocolate chips until melted.

Add confectioner's sugar, vanilla, and nuts (if using). With wooden spoon beat until thick and glossy. Spread in prepared 8" pan. Refrigerate 2 hours or until firm. Cut into 1" squares.

Grandma Greenlaw's Hermits

½ cup shortening
1 cup molasses
1 cup sugar
1 egg
½ teaspoon ground cloves
½ teaspoon salt
1 cup raisin
½ cup milk
1 teaspoon ground allspice
1 teaspoon ground cinnamon
1 teaspoon ground nutmeg
1½ teaspoons baking soda
4 cups flour

Combine all ingredients and mix well. Drop by spoonfuls onto greased cookie sheet. Bake 15 minutes in 375° oven. Best to undercook these cookies than over cook them, so watch the first batch.

Blueberry Pie

¾ cup sugar
3 tablespoons cornstarch
pinch salt
2 tablespoons cold water
2 tablespoons fresh lemon juice
1 tablespoon butter
1 tablespoon lemon peel – grated
6 cups fresh or frozen blueberries
1 Pie Crust (see recipe)

Make crust according to pie dough recipe. Roll out bottom and place in pie pan. Cover with plastic wrap and refrigerate for 30 minutes.

Whisk sugar, cornstarch, and salt together in a medium saucepan. Add water and lemon juice, whisking until smooth. Add butter and lemon peel. Add 2 cups of blueberries and mash coarsely with a potato masher. Cook over medium heat until mixture begins to thicken and boils. Make sure to watch and stir this mixture often. Add remaining blueberries and bring back to a boil. Remove from heat and pour into prepared pie shell.

Moisten edge of the bottom crust. Roll out the top crust and place over blueberry mixture. Trim to ½" larger than pie pan. Press edges firmly together, roll edges under, flute, then slash in the center of the crust. Sprinkle with sugar.

Bake in a 425° oven for 15 minutes, then turn down to 400° and continue baking for 25 minutes. Make sure to check on pie to ensure top does not over brown. If it does, then cover with foil.

Remove from the oven, place pie on rack to cool.

Chocolate Chip Cookies

1⅔ cups flour
1¼ teaspoons baking soda
¾ teaspoon baking powder
¼ teaspoon salt
1 cup butter
¾ cup sugar
⅔ cup light brown sugar – packed
1 large egg
1½ tablespoons milk
2½ teaspoons vanilla
1⅓ cups rolled oats – ground fine in a blender
1 cup semisweet chocolate chips
3 ounces milk chocolate bar – coarsely chopped
¾ cup chopped walnuts or pecans

Whisk together the flour, baking soda, baking powder, and salt. Set aside.

With an electric mixer, beat the butter until fluffy and smooth, about 3 minutes. Add the sugars, egg, milk, and vanilla until well combined.

Add the flour mixture to the butter mixture until well combined. Stir in the oat flour, chocolate chips, milk chocolate bar, and nuts, if using.

Drop by rounded tablespoon or shape dough into 1½ inch balls. Place on greased cookies sheets 2 inches apart.

Bake for 8 to 10 minutes, or until just brown. Do not overbake, they will continue to bake as you cool them on the cookie sheets. Transfer sheets to cooling racks and let cookies cool on sheets for 3 to 4 minutes. Then transfer cookies to wire racks until completely cool.

Pie Crust (double crusts)

2 cups flour
1 tablespoon sugar
¾ cup Crisco
pinch of salt
1 cup ice water
1½ teaspoon white vinegar

Whisk together flour, sugar, and salt. With a pastry blender or two forks cut in the Crisco until the mixture resembles small peas. Add the vinegar to the ice water and stir. Then slowly add half the water to the mixture. Stir to combine. If the dough is dry, add a tablespoon of water at a time until the dough forms a moist ball. I usually make my dough wetter than most people do. Divide the dough into 2 disks. Wrap them in plastic wrap and place in a Ziploc bag and refrigerate. Refrigerate for at least 1 hour before attempting to roll out.

You can leave this dough in the fridge for up to 2 days if well sealed.

Desserts

....

Pecan Tartlets

1 cup butter
1 8 ounce package cream cheese – softened
3 tablespoons sugar
½ teaspoon vanilla
2¼ cups flour
7 ounces pecans – chopped
2 eggs
2 cups light brown sugar – packed
2 tablespoons butter – melted
1 teaspoon vanilla
1 pinch salt
4 ounces pecans – toasted and chopped

Using an electric mixer beat together butter, cream cheese, sugar, vanilla, and a pinch of salt in a large bowl. Beat until light and fluffy, about 3 minutes. Reduce speed to low and add flour. Remove and wrap in plastic wrap. Chill until firm, approximately 1 hour.

After 1 hour, take dough out of refrigerator and make 1 inch balls. Place in well greased mini tart pans, using a tart tamper, press down in the centers so that the dough fits the cups snugly.

Sprinkle chopped pecans in the bottom of each mini tart.

Beat eggs slightly with a fork. Then add sugar, melted butter, vanilla, and salt. Pour this mixture into a pitcher or a measuring cup with a spout.

Fill mini tarts until two thirds full. Top each with toasted pecans. Bake at 350° for 30 minutes or until golden.

Chocolate Crackle Cookies

1 cup semisweet chocolate
1 cup brown sugar – packed
⅓ cup canola oil
2 eggs
1 teaspoon vanilla
1 cup flour
1 teaspoon baking powder
¼ teaspoon salt
1 cup powdered sugar

Melt chocolate and then combine with sugar and oil. Add eggs one at a time and beat well after each addition. Add vanilla.

Combine flour, baking powder, and salt in a medium bowl. Whisk to remove any lumps.

Add flour mixture to chocolate mixture until well combined. Chill dough for 30 minutes.

Roll dough into 1" balls, then into powdered sugar to coat. Place on greased cookie sheet. Bake at 350° for 10 to 12 minutes. Do not over bake. Cool on a rack.

Tips from Chef Val

Tartlet dough can be tricky, but don't give up. Roll into small one-inch balls and place in the mini-muffin tins. Then, using a tart tamper, press evenly to form a crust. If you don't have a tart tamper, use a wooden dowel.

Desserts

Apple Pie

1 Pie Crust (see recipe)
1¼ cups sugar
½ teaspoon salt
1 tablespoon ground cinnamon
¾ tablespoon ground nutmeg
2 tablespoons flour
6 Granny Smith apples – cored, peeled,
   and sliced
6 Braebern apples – cored, peeled,
   and sliced
1 teaspoon lemon rind – grated
1½ tablespoons butter – softened

Preheat oven to 425°.

Prepare bottom crust and place in a greased pie pan. Cover with plastic wrap and then place in refrigerator for 1 hour.

Mix dry ingredients together in a medium size bowl. Whisk to remove any lumps.

Peel and core apples and then slice apples using a food processor or by hand. Place in a large bowl. Pour dry ingredient mixture over the apples and mix well. I like to use my hands to ensure every apple slice is coated. Place apple mixture into pastry lined pie pan until pan is filled.

Sprinkle with lemon rind and dot with butter.

Moisten edge of bottom crust.

Roll top crust and then place over apple filling. Then trim to ½" larger than pie pan. Press edges firmly together, roll edges under, flute, and slash vents in the center of the crust. Sprinkle with sugar.

Bake at 425° for 15 minutes. Then turn oven down to 400° and bake for another 45-60 minutes. Check after 35 minutes to ensure crust is not too browned. If it is, cover with foil. I would check pie every 15 minutes to prevent over browning.

NOTE: I sometimes make several pies at a time, freezing one. Then when I need a pie I just remove the pie from the freezer and pop it in the oven, baking at 425° for 30 minutes. Then turn oven down to 400° and bake for another hour. Again checking to ensure the crust is not browning too much.

Pistachio Freeze

1 20 ounce can crushed pineapple
1 .3 ounce box pistachio instant pudding
1 8 ounce container of cool whip
½ cup nuts – chopped
½ cup maraschino cherries

Mix together pineapple with pudding. Add cool whip, then add cherries and nuts. Freeze. Serve sliced.

Desserts

....

Dark Chocolate Truffles

⅔ cup heavy cream
8 ounces semisweet chocolate – chopped
    into ¼" pieces
4 ounces unsweetened chocolate – chopped
    into ¼" pieces
2 tablespoons unsweetened cocoa – sifted
2 tablespoons confectioners sugar – sifted

Heat the heavy cream in a large saucepan over medium heat. Bring to a boil. Pour the boiling cream over the chocolate. Allow to stand 5 minutes, then stir until smooth (now you have ganache). Refrigerate the ganache for 1 hour until firm but not hard.

Line a baking sheet with parchment paper. Using a 1 ounce cookie scoop, scoop into ganache for each truffle. Place each evenly spaced on baking sheet. Refrigerate 15 minutes. When the ganache is firm enough to handle, remove from the refrigerator and individually roll each portion of ganache in your palms, using just enough pressure to form smooth rounds. Roll 16 of the rounds in 2 tablespoons cocoa and separately roll 8 in the confectioners sugar until completely covered.

Store the truffles in a tightly sealed plastic container, in the refrigerator.

Remove about 1 hour before serving.

Sugar Pecans

½ cup butter
1 pound pecans – unsalted
2 egg whites
1 cup sugar
dash salt

Preheat oven to 325°. Using a pan with sides, melt the butter in the oven.

Pour pecans into a large mixing bowl. In a small mixing bowl stir egg whites, sugar, and salt together. Pour over pecans and mix until well coated. Spread pecan mixture evenly in the melted butter.

Bake for 30-45 minutes, stirring every 10 minutes. Remove to another cookie sheet to cool. Store in a cool place. Will freeze for up to 6 months.

MENU IDEAS
....

Dessert Party

Macaroons

Apricot Chocolate Cookies

Mini Chocolate Cheesecakes

Chocolate Fudge

Sugar Pecans

Peanut Butter Balls

Lemon Tart

1¼ cups flour
4 teaspoons sugar
⅛ teaspoon salt
½ cup butter – cold
1 large egg yolk
1 tablespoon milk
4 eggs
1½ cups sugar
½ cup orange juice
½ cup lemon juice
1 lemon – zested
1 orange – zested
¼ cup heavy cream

In a food processor, pulse together the flour, sugar, and salt. Cut the butter into small pieces and add to processor, pulsing until the mixture resembles coarse meal. Beat the egg yolk with 1 tablespoon milk, and then add to the flour mixture. Pulse until the dough forms a ball. Remove and wrap in plastic wrap. Flatten into a disk shape and place in refrigerator for several hours or overnight.

Remove dough from fridge and let soften slightly. Then roll the dough into a 13" round on a slightly floured surface. Fit the dough into a 10½" tart pan with a removable bottom. Trim the dough to ½" greater than the pan edge, fold over excess and press into the tart pan. Freeze the tart shell until firm, about 20 minutes.

Preheat oven to 350°.

Line the shell with foil and fill with pie weights, rice, or dried beans. Bake for 20 minutes. Remove the foil and weights and bake an additional 10 to 15 minutes, until lightly golden. Remove the shell from the oven.

While the pastry is baking and almost done, make the filling. Whisk together the eggs, sugar, orange juice, lemon juice, lemon zest, orange zest, and cream until smooth.

Transfer the tart shell to a preheated 350° oven. Pour the filling slowly into the shell as high as possible without overfilling.

Bake the tart for 25 minutes or until the filling is barely set. Check the tart after 20 minutes and keep checking every few minutes. It is extremely important not to over bake this filling.

Cool to room temperature before serving.

Fresh Apple Cake

1½ cups canola oil
2 cups sugar
3 eggs
1 teaspoon vanilla
3 cups flour
1 teaspoon baking soda
1 teaspoon ground nutmeg
½ teaspoon salt
2 teaspoons ground cinnamon
3 cups apples – cored, peeled, and diced
1 cup nuts – chopped
1 cup raisin
1 cup light brown sugar
¼ cup milk
½ cup margarine
1 teaspoon vanilla

Mix oil, sugar, eggs, and vanilla together. Set aside.

Whisk dry ingredients together. Mix with egg mixture. Add apples, nuts, and raisins and combine well. Pour into a greased and floured tube pan. Bake for 1½ hours at 300°.

For the glaze: Mix together the brown sugar, milk, margarine, and vanilla in a medium saucepan over medium high heat. Boil for 2 minutes. Pour over warm cake. The glaze soaks into the cake making for a very rich cake.

. . . .

Momma's Cherry Pie

1 Pie Crust (see recipe)
5 14½ ounce cans red cherries – save liquid
½ cup sugar
⅛ teaspoon salt
1½ tablespoons cornstarch
3 tablespoons flour
4 drops almond extract
2 drops red food coloring

Line pie pan with pastry. Drain cherries, saving liquid. Taste the cherries, if they are not sweet, plan on adding more sugar, anywhere from ¼ - ½ cup more sugar. Mix sugar, salt, cornstarch, and flour together in saucepan, blend in juice from cherries (¾ cup). Cook over medium heat, stirring constantly until mixture boils and thickens. Remove from heat, add almond extract, cherries, and red food coloring. Pour cherry mixture into pastry lined pan.

Roll out pastry for upper crust, cut a design for steam vents. Moisten edge of lower crust with water, lay upper crust over and press together. Trim, roll edges under, flute, and let rest for 10 minutes in refrigerator. Sprinkle with sugar.

Bake in a 450° oven for 15 minutes until crust is lightly browned, then reduce heat to 325° and continue baking 15 minutes longer.

Cool before cutting.

Coconut Brownies

1 Brownie Mix
⅓ cup vegetable oil
⅓ cup water
1 egg
1 teaspoon salt
1 14 ounce bag shredded coconut
1 cup sweetened condensed milk
2 large egg whites
1 tablespoon flour
1½ teaspoons vanilla
⅛ teaspoon baking powder

Combine brownie mix with oil, water, and egg. Pour into a greased 8" square pan. Bake at 350° for 20 minutes. Mix together salt, coconut, condensed milk, egg whites, flour, vanilla extract, and baking powder. Remove brownies from the oven after 20 minutes and spoon the coconut mixture evenly over the brownies. Return brownies to the oven and bake for another 20 to 30 minutes. Coconut should be golden brown. Cool. Cut into squares.

Lemon Cheesecake

1 8 ounce bag Nabisco's Barnum
   Animal Crackers
3 tablespoons sugar
4 tablespoons unsalted butter – melted
1¼ cups sugar
1 tablespoon lemon zest
3 8 ounce packages Philadelphia Cream Cheese
   room temperature and cut into 1" pieces
4 large eggs – room temperature
¼ cup lemon juice
2 teaspoons vanilla extract
¼ teaspoon salt
½ cup heavy cream
1 Lemon Curd (see recipe)

Oven rack should be a lowest setting possible. Preheat oven to 325°.

In a food processor, add cookies and process until a fine crumb occurs. Add 3 tablespoons of sugar and pulse 2 to 3 times to combine. Then add warm melted butter in a slow steady stream while continuing to pulse. Mixture should resemble wet sand when done. Transfer to a 9" springform pan. Use a dry measuring cup, evenly press crumbs into the sides and around bottom. Bake in oven for 15 minutes, until golden brown. Cool on a wire rack for at least 30 minutes.

Process ¼ cup sugar and lemon zest in food processor, until sugar is yellow and zest is ground into a fine sugar. This will take about 15 seconds. Add remaining 1 cup sugar and pulse until it resembles a fine sugar.

Beat cream cheese with an electric mixer to soften, about 5 seconds. While machine is running add sugar mixture. Continue to beat until mixture is creamy and smooth, making sure to scrap down sides of bowl.

Add eggs two at a time while mixer is on low. Making sure to scrap sides and bottom after each addition.

Add lemon juice, vanilla, and salt. Mix until just incorporated, about 5 seconds. Add cream and mix until combined, about 5 more seconds.

Give batter a final scrapping, stirring with spatula. Then pour batter into prepared springform pan.

Bake until center jiggles slightly, sides just start to puff, and surface is no longer shiny. This should take about 60 minutes. Turn oven off and prop open oven door with a wooden clothes pin or the handle of a wooden spoon and allow cheesecake to cool in the oven for 1 hour.

Transfer cake to wire rack. Run a knife around edges to loosen and cool cake at room temperature for about 2 hours.

When cake is cool, spread Lemon Curd onto cheesecake while cake is still in the springform pan. Using an off set spatula will ensure that the Lemon Curd is spread evenly over the top. Cover tightly with plastic wrap and refrigerate for at least 4 hours or up to 24.

To serve remove sides of springform pan and cut into wedges.

Tips from Chef Val

Want smaller bites of chocolate or lemon cheesecakes? You can make mini cakes out of them by using mini-muffin pans. Follow the recipe. Just reduce baking time to 20-30 minutes.

Desserts

· ·

Peach Tart

1½ cups all purpose flour
3 tablespoons sugar
¼ teaspoon salt
½ cup chilled unsalted butter
3½ tablespoons ice water
½ cup sugar
6 tablespoons flour
2 tablespoons lemon zest
2 24 ounce jars fresh sliced
   peaches – drained
4 tablespoons honey
4 tablespoons chilled unsalted butter –
   cut into small pieces
4 tablespoons sliced almonds
4 tablespoons peach preserves – melted
¼ cup fresh or frozen blueberries (optional)
whipped cream

Combine first 3 ingredients in a food processor, pulse for 3 seconds. Add butter in small pieces and pulse until dough resembles pea size pieces. With machine running add enough ice water by tablespoonfuls to form moist clumps. Dump dough onto plastic wrap, flatten into a disk. Wrap and refrigerate at least 1 hour. This can be done up to 2 days in advance.

Roll out dough on a lightly floured surface to approximately 12" round. Transfer to a greased tart pan with a removable bottom. Trim dough to 1" over the edge and then fold over and press to form a double thick side. Press inside edge of crust to tart pan. Dock bottom of crust with fork. Refrigerate 1 hour.

Preheat oven to 400°. Bake tart crust until golden, piercing with a fork if bubbles form. Bake for 25 minutes. This can be made a day in advance, just make sure to cool, then wrap in plastic and keep at room temperature.

For the filling, mix the sugar, flour, and lemon zest in a large bowl. Add peaches and toss to coat. Add blueberries if using. Pour into baked tart crust. Drizzle honey over peach mixture. Dot with butter and sprinkle with almonds. Bake for 35 minutes. Brush fruit and almonds with peach preserves.

Cool 15 minutes before serving.

Top with whipped cream.

Peanut Butter Balls

1 box powdered sugar
½ cup margarine or butter – at
 room temperature
¼ teaspoon salt
1 teaspoon vanilla
1 cup peanut butter
3 tablespoons milk
16 ounces chocolate chips
1 teaspoon vegetable shortening

Beat sugar, margarine or butter, salt, and vanilla together until smooth. Add the peanut butter and milk to make mixture soft. Roll into small balls using your hands or a melon baller. Place on a wax paper lined cookie sheet and place in freezer for 30 minutes.

Melt chocolate chips and vegetable shortening in a double boiler. Dip peanut butter balls into melted chocolate using two spoons. Place on a cookie sheet lined with wax paper. Place cookie sheet in freezer for at least 1 hour.

Remove peanut butter balls from freezer and store in Ziploc baggies in the refrigerator until ready to eat.

Peanut Butter Cookies

1 cup butter
2 cups sugar
½ cup brown sugar – packed
3 large eggs
½ cups peanut butter
¾ teaspoon vanilla
2¼ cups flour
¾ teaspoon baking soda
¼ teaspoon salt
1 cup peanuts – coarsely chopped
1 cup white chocolate bits (optional)

Preheat the oven to 350°. Mix together the butter and sugars until light and fluffy, about 3 minutes. Add eggs one at a time. Scrap down the sides then add the peanut butter and vanilla.

Whisk together the flour, baking soda, and salt. Add to the peanut butter mixture. Add the coarsely chopped peanuts and white chocolate, if using.

Using a tablespoon drop the cookies onto a cookie sheet. Bake on middle oven rack 10 to 12 minutes. Cool for 1 minute on cookie sheet, then transfer to wire racks to cool.

Macaroons

14 ounces Bakers Angel Flake Coconut
1 14 ounce can Sweetened condensed milk
2 teaspoons vanilla

Heat oven to 350°.

Mix coconut, milk, and vanilla in a large bowl.

Drop by teaspoonful onto well greased cookie sheets. Bake for 10-12 minutes. Let cool and remove to wire racks to completely cool.

Tips from Chef Val

To prevent your pie crust from overbrowning, take a foil pie tin, cut out the bottom and use the ring for the pie edge.

Desciption

....

Pear Upside Down Cake

8 tablespoons unsalted butter
¾ cup packed light brown sugar – packed
3 ripe pears – cored, peeled, and sliced
1½ cups all-purpose flour
1 teaspoon baking powder
2 teaspoons salt
8 tablespoons unsalted butter
1 cup granulated sugar
1 teaspoon pure vanilla extract
2 large eggs – separated
½ cup whole milk
¼ teaspoon cream of tartar

Melt the butter in the bottom of a 10" cast-iron skillet over a low heat. Add the brown sugar, stirring until dissolved. Swirl to coat the entire bottom. Remove from heat. Cut the pears into ¼" slices and arrange them in a circular pattern over the brown-sugar mixture.

Preheat the oven to 350°. To make the cake batter, in a medium bowl whisk together the flour, baking powder, and salt.

In the bowl of an electric mixer, cream the butter and sugar on medium speed until light and fluffy about 3 minutes. Add the vanilla extract then the egg yolks, one at a time, mixing well after each addition.

Alternating with the milk, gradually add the flour mixture to the butter mixture, and mix on low speed, until the flour is incorporated.

In a large bowl, beat the egg whites and the cream of tarter with a mixer until stiff, but not dry. Using a rubber spatula, fold egg whites into the batter. Transfer to skillet. Using an offset spatula, spread the batter evenly over the pears.

Bake until well browned on top and a cake tester comes out clean, about 45 minutes. Run a knife around the inside of the pan, and immediately invert the cake onto a serving dish. Serve warm or at room temperature.

Red & White Cookies

1 cup unsalted butter – room temperature
2 cups sugar
1 large egg
½ cup sour cream
3 cups all purpose flour
¼ teaspoon baking powder
¼ teaspoon salt
1 cup currants
3 tablespoons freshly grated lemon zest
1 teaspoon lemon extract

Preheat oven to 350°. In the bowl of an electric mixer, beat the butter and sugar until light and fluffy about 3 minutes. Add the egg and beat to combine. Beat in sour cream.

In a medium bowl, whisk together the flour, baking powder, and salt. Add the currants and lemon zest, and stir to combine. Combine with the butter mixture. Add the lemon extract, beat to combine.

Using a tablespoon, drop the cookies onto a cookie sheet. Bake until puffed and golden around the edges, about 10 minutes. Cool 5 minutes on cookie sheets, then move to rack to cool completely.

Pumpkin Pie

1½ cups brown sugar
1 cup canned pumpkin
⅔ cup vegetable oil
2 eggs
¼ cup water
2 cups all purpose flour
1 teaspoon salt
½ teaspoon ground cinnamon
½ teaspoon ground nutmeg
½ teaspoon ground ginger
1 unbaked Pie Crust (see recipe)

Combine first 10 ingredients until smooth. Place in unbaked pie shell. Bake in 425° oven for 15 minutes. Lower temperature to 350° and continue baking about 35 minutes or until custard is firm. Cool and serve.

Double Chocolate Drops

1⅓ cups vegetable shortening
1 cup sugar
⅔ cup brown sugar – packed
3 tablespoons milk
1 tablespoon vanilla
2 eggs
2¼ cups flour
⅔ cup unsweetened cocoa
1 teaspoon baking soda
1 teaspoon salt
1½ cups broken walnuts
1 cup semisweet chocolate chip

Preheat the oven to 350°. Cream shortening, sugars, milk, and vanilla in a large bowl at medium speed of an electric mixer. Add eggs one at a time. Beat well after each addition and scrap down the sides of the bowl after each addition.

Whisk together flour, cocoa, baking soda, and salt. Add to creamed mixture. Stir in nuts and chips. Drop heaping tablespoon of dough onto ungreased cookie sheet 2" apart.

Bake 9-11 minutes. Cool 2 minutes on cookie sheet. Remove to cooling rack.

Vanilla Ice Cream

2 cups milk
¼ cup sugar
½ cup condensed milk
½ cup heavy cream
2 teaspoons pure vanilla
pinch salt

Mix in blender all ingredients. Refrigerate overnight. Then follow directions on your ice cream machine.

Desserts

Sour Cream Coffee Cake

¾ cup light brown sugar – packed
½ cup flour
1½ teaspoons ground cinnamon
¼ teaspoon salt
1 tablespoon lemon rind – grated
3 tablespoons butter, cold – cut into 1" cubes
¾ cup walnuts or pecans – chopped
1½ sticks butter – room temperature
1½ cups sugar
3 large eggs
1½ teaspoons vanilla extract
1¼ cups sour cream
2½ cups cake flour
2 teaspoons baking powder
½ teaspoon baking soda
½ teaspoon salt
½ cup powdered sugar
2 tablespoons milk
1 teaspoon vanilla extract

Preheat oven to 350°. Grease and flour a bundt pan.

For the streusel, place the brown sugar, flour, cinnamon, salt, lemon rind, and butter in a bowl and using pastry blender, combine until mixture resembles corn meal. Mix in nuts. Spoon half of streusel in bunt pan. Set aside.

Cream the butter and sugar until light and fluffy, about 3 minutes. Add the eggs one at a time and scrape down the sides of the bowl after each addition. Add vanilla and sour cream, continue to beat until well combined.

In a separate bowl whisk flour, baking powder, baking soda, and salt together. With the mixer on very low, add the flour to the butter mixture until combined. Remove from mixer and stir to ensure all is well combined.

Spoon half the batter over the streusel, using an offset spatula to ensure evenness. Sprinkle remaining streusel over the batter evenly. Then spread remaining batter over streusel.

Bake for 50 minutes or until a cake tester comes out clean.

Let cool for 30 minutes on wire rack before inverting. Serve streusel side up.

Whisk powdered sugar, vanilla extract, and milk together to make a runny glaze. Drizzle over the cake.

Menu Ideas

Dinner Party

Party Pumps

Chicken in Champagne
& Mushroom Sauce

Mashed Potatoes

Green Bean Delight

Momma's Cherry Pie

Desserts

Lemon Tartlets

5 tablespoons cold butter – cut into 1" cubes
1 cup flour
3 tablespoons sugar
1 large egg yolk
1 teaspoon vanilla extract
1 teaspoon lemon zest – grated
pinch of salt
1 8 ounce package Philadelphia Cream Cheese
  – room temperature and cut into 1" pieces
⅓ cup sugar
1 large egg – room temperature
3 tablespoons lemon zest – grated
1 tablespoon lemon juice
½ teaspoon vanilla extract
cooking spray

Preheat oven to 350°. Spray mini-muffin pans with cooking spray. Set aside.

In a food processor, add the flour and butter until a fine even crumb occurs. Add the sugar, egg yolk, vanilla, lemon zest, and salt. Pulse to combine. Shape dough into 1" balls and place each ball into the muffin cup. Using a tart tamper, press down in the centers so that the dough fits the cups snugly.

Bake until lightly browned, 15 to 20 minutes. Transfer pans to a wire rack to cool.

Using an electric mixer beat the cream cheese, sugar, egg, lemon zest and juice, and vanilla until very smooth. Pour this mixture into a pitcher or a measuring cup with a spout. Fill the cooled crusts.

Bake at 350° for 10 to 12 minutes. Transfer the tartlets to a wire rack to cool.

The tartlets can be stored in the refrigerator in an airtight container for up to 3 days.

Strawberry Rhubarb Pie

1 pint strawberries – washed and sliced
1 quart rhubarb
1¼ cups sugar
2 tablespoons tapioca
1 teaspoon orange peel – grated
2 tablespoons flour
1 tablespoon butter
1 Pie Crust (see recipe)

Chop rhubarb into ¼" dice. Mix rhubarb, sugar, tapioca, and orange peel in a large bowl. Let stand 15 minutes.

Place 1 of the pie crusts in 9" pie pan. Fill with fruit mixture, dot with butter. Cover with remaining pie crust. Moisten and seal edges, trim, roll edges under, and flute. Sprinkle with sugar. Cut several slits in top crust to permit steam to escape.

Bake at 425° for 20 minutes, then lower heat to 350° and continue to bake for 1 hour and 25 minutes.

Index

Index

Index

Index

Index

Index

F

Fruit

Index

Index

Index

Index

Index

Book
Ordering
Information

....

Give the gift of **"Personal Chef Secrets"** to your family and friends.
Check your local Bookstore or order here.

Please send me ____ copies of **"Personal Chef Secrets"** for $19.95 each.

Include $3.95 shipping and handling for one book, and $1.95 for each additional
book. Colorado residents must include applicable sales tax.

Please charge my   ☐ Visa   ☐ Mastercard   ☐ AmEx   ☐ Discover

Card Number _____

Name on the Card _____

Exp. Date: _____

Name _____

Address _____

City _____ State _____ Zip _____

Phone _____

Email _____

Payment must accompany orders. Allow 3 weeks for delivery.